LAPTOP MUSIC

Create, record, perform, or just listen to, music on your laptop computer

PC Publishing

PC Publishing
Keeper's House
Merton
Thetford
Norfolk IP25 6QH
UK

Tel 01953 889900
Fax 01953 889901
email info@pc-publishing.com
web site http://www.pc-publishing.com

First published 2004

© PC Publishing

ISBN 1870775 89 9

British Library Cataloguing in Publication Data
A catalogue record for this book is available from the British Library

Printed and bound in Great Britain by Biddles, King's Lynn, Norfolk

Thanks to

The short version

Thanks to everybody who helped with this book!

The long version

For supplying test material: Isabelle Alran and Lucy Ansell at M-Audio for the FW410, Reason 2.5, Ozone, and Studiopack; Bil Bryant at PowerFX for samples – on CD, DVD, and online; Michael Carroll and Jorg Hüttner at Celemony for the superb Melodyne 2; Zhi Liu at Arboretum for Montage; Colin Meager at Evolution for the MK keyboards and UC controllers; Jeremy Sagan at Sagan Tech for Metro 6; Risto Sampola at Arbiter for Native Instruments and Steinberg applications; Jules Storer at Raw Material Software for Tracktion; Ted Weil at Bitheadz for Session, Synth Expander and Phrazer.

See the 'links' section at the end of the book for full contact information.

Thanks to all the laptop musicians who allowed me to interview them in person, or who completed my email questionnaire; there'd be no book without your valued feedback…keep on, er, rockin.

Obviously I'm totally impartial and would never dream of singling out anybody for special mention, so … a special mention to the girls and boys of the Brighton/London Laptop Jammers – their enthusiasm and willingness to accommodate newbies makes them a great example for any group of musicians/artists. Considering that they're working in such a technological realm, they do an impressive job of remaining focused on having fun with music and video, instead of disappearing down obscure academic and technical paths …

Personal thanks to Jan Anderson, Grace Connor, and mindlobster for their assistance and support during the house moves (four), health problems and various other personal crises that occurred during the writing of this book … and of course to the ever-patient Phil Chapman at PC Publishing for giving me the chance to write it in the first place…please can I go to sleep now?

About the interviews

P erhaps unusually for a book of this type, *Laptop Music* contains many quotes drawn from interviews. Furthermore, most of the interviews are with people who are somewhat less than household names – that's putting it politely – you probably won't have heard of them.

I didn't want this book to read as if its contents derived exclusively from internet research and press releases; or as a giant ad for one particular product; or as a substitute for a manual that should have been in the box in the first place. Laptop music needs different treatment because it's a different type of subject, a distinct entity separate from the 'regular' studio-bound world of computer music; it has a more human element. This was borne out by the positive response I received from the worldwide laptop community. The internet is full of places to get facts and figures about software and hardware performance, and places to get help with specific problems or to discuss specific issues, but there isn't a book that gathers together the different threads of computer geekery, music making, and sociability that define the strange phenomenon of laptop music.

I interviewed a lot of people for this book – people from different countries and backgrounds. There are many common challenges faced by laptop musicians, but the responses to these challenges vary enormously. It's amazing how people can reach such different conclusions based on the same circumstances.

The most important difference between laptops and desktops is that laptops actually encourage somebody to venture out into the physical world beyond the bedroom or studio, instead of remaining deskbound and secluded; it can be a 'physical' social activity rather than a 'virtual' social activity ... the Laptop Jams in Brighton and London exemplify this. People get together ... it's about going out...the laptop becomes a portable instrument like a guitar or a keyboard, not a means to keep the world at arm's length. If you go out to a cafe or other public space with a laptop, and if you're doing something that looks interesting maybe using Propellerhead Reason or Ableton Live or some other eye-catching application, then chances are that somebody will come up to you and check out what you're doing ... maybe they're already a laptop user, or thinking about becoming a laptop user ... it's such a great change if you're used to the isolation of the studio ... you have to welcome it and not be irritated at the interruption, you can learn something from talking to these curious people.

This human interaction is why the interviews are here; it's an important aspect of laptop music. It's something you need to know just as much as you need to know what 'bus powered' or 'built-in obsolescence' mean. Welcome to the world!

Credits

The interviews with Black Eyed Peas, Charlie Clouser, Crystal Method, Mijk Van Dijk, Monolake, DJ Rabuake, and Tom Scott are quoted with permission from www.m-audio.co.uk.

Alesis AirFX photo courtesy of Alesis.
Alphabet Soup screenshot courtesy of Oz Music Code.
Aluminium case photo courtesy of Aluminium Case Company.
Apple product photos courtesy of Apple.
Belkin product photos courtesy of Belkin Corporation.
Chapman Stick photos courtesy of Stick Enterprises.
Continuum Fingerboard photo courtesy of Twelfth Root.
Contour Shuttle photos courtesy of Contour Design Inc.
Crumpler bag photo courtesy of JOBO USA.
David Das photos courtesy of David Das.
Digital Media Remote photo courtesy of Keyspan.
Echo Indigo photos courtesy of Arbiter Group.
Edirol product photos courtesy of Edirol.
Evolution product photos courtesy of Evolution.
Final Scratch photos courtesy of Stanton Magnetics.
Fog Screen photo courtesy of Fog Screen Inc.
GDAM screenshot courtesy of Dave Benson and Geoff Matters.
Gigaport photo courtesy of Ego Systems Inc.
Griffin Technology product photos courtesy of Griffin Technology.
Hammerfall DSP Multiface photo courtesy of RME.
Hewlett Packard and Compaq laptop photos courtesy of Hewlett Packard.
JL Cooper CS-32 photo courtesy JL Cooper Electronics.
Kensington USB light photos courtesy of Kensington Technology Group.
Kenton Midistream photos courtesy of Kenton Electronics.
Lacie product photos courtesy of Lacie.
M-Audio product photos courtesy of M-Audio.
MBox photo and ProTools screenshots courtesy of Digidesign UK.
Mini-Me photo courtesy of Apogee Electronics.
MOTU 828 photos courtesy of MusicTrack.
Nanoloop screenshot courtesy of Oliver Wittchow.
Orange Micro Combo photo courtesy of Orange Micro Inc.
Pluggo and Max/MSP screenshots courtesy of Cycling74.

Contents

Introduction

This book is obsolete ... and cool. Instant retro: by the time you read this, this book will be out of date.

That's not an editorial suicide note designed to make you (a) decide not to buy this book, or (b) if you've bought it already, angrily race back to your book store demanding a refund; it's simply a reflection of how fast the laptop music scene is changing. Inevitably, because this book was written and printed and distributed over a period of months rather than days, hours, or even minutes, a large proportion of the hardware and software featured will have been upgraded, updated, or rendered totally obsolete. Nonetheless, this book will continue to be useful and relevant, with a far longer lifespan than some of the products described within its pages, providing an overview of the types of gear available, but also (more important) sensible advice, biased opinions, real-world techniques, useful links, and other assorted coverage of the booming laptop music scene – the geeks, freaks, and computer chic that might be delineating an underground electro-folk revolution, or might just be playing with the high cost hula hoop of the future. No matter what your level of interest and experience, if you own a laptop or plan to buy one, this book is cool!

Fundamentally the laptop has the potential to take art, in all areas, out of the studio and into the world in a very big way. Ergo Phizmiz (performer/ composer)

What is laptop music?

What is 'laptop music'? Is it a genre? Is it a lifestyle? Does the term mean anything at all? If you go to www.laptopmusic.com you will find a site dedicated to Suzuki's OmniChord and QChord, guitar-style instant music devices for the home/amateur market; that can't be right!

We've got to get this thing going, so for now let's just agree that 'laptop music' covers all music-related activities that happen on laptop computers – performing, recording, composing, and just plain listening. These awkward definition-type questions will re surface later though – it's unavoidable, because, more so on laptops than on desktop computers, there is a tremendous amount of crossover between the previously mentioned activities.

And ... let's also agree that a 'laptop' is a portable computer which can run from battery power, with screen sizes typically ranging from a dinky 12 inches to a whopping 17 inches.

There are other portable computing options of course: mobile phones, PDAs (personal digital assistants – electronic organisers, to you and I, usually featuring

What is laptop music? It's just the next evolution of working on computer-based music. David Das (performer/producer)

the Palm OS or a version of Windows), and sub-notebooks – computers with very small screens, usually too small to be suitable for music use unless you're an eye-ball masochist with a scroll wheel fetish.

And there are of course other battery-driven electronic music options: sequencers, samplers, and even portastudio-style digital recorders that are small enough to fit in a (big) pocket – usually quite basic in function, but interesting nevertheless.

It's possible to find a musical use for all of the above gadgets, though they don't really fit into the accepted realm of 'laptop music'... they will reappear briefly later in Chapter 8.

What this book is for – in case you're still wondering

This book *won't* give you detailed how to's for every bit of software on the planet, or present comprehensive hardware shootouts in a 'Mac versus PC' way. Nor will it explain commonly used music technology terms such as 'MIDI', nor will it give comprehensive performance statistics about dark technical things that go on inside computers; mysterious things like bus and cache and IRQ.

The aim of this book is simple. To help laptop musicians – wannabes or diehards – appreciate their computer's technical and creative potential. I'll be doing this by looking at the tools available, and by talking to other laptop musicians about how and why they do what they do. I wanted laptop musicians to share their experiences and feelings about the subject, to pass on what they've learned so far.

Hopefully everybody should find something worthwhile in this, whether it's technical information or inspiration – it's time to make the most of your expensive qwerty noise maker!

I've tried to organise this book according to the musical situations in which you might be using your laptop, and what laptop-specific gear and attitudes you might need to get the job done. You know what I'm talking about:

Hardware

Audio interfaces, MIDI interfaces, audio/MIDI interfaces, external storage devices, and MIDI controllers such as keyboards and mixers, as well as the various goofier accessories that·pop up from time to time. Being the tightly packed little gadgets they are, laptops aren't so easy to expand or upgrade as their deskbound relatives, so external expansion is usually the way to go, connected via FireWire or USB. Given that the true spirit of laptop use lies in the portability it offers, and the 'in-the-field' quality of the experience, I'm *very* biased towards devices which are bus-powered; that is, they take their power from connection with the computer rather than needing a nasty big mains power supply. A fully battery-powered set-up means that you can work at home and 'on the road' (a glamorous term usually describing something somewhat less than glamorous) with exactly the same configuration, so you don't feel like you've left something behind.

Software

Modern laptops are powerful enough to run more or less any software that will run on a desktop computer, and there are very few applications optimised solely for lap-top use. However, there are applications which tend not to be suitable for laptop use, for instance those that benefit from large displays (more traditionally designed sequencers and video editors tend to be the worst culprits), or those that make excessive demands on processor power and memory (usually the latest 'cutting edge' products – you know, the things you really want), or those applications that require close integration with bulky mains powered external hardware interfaces.

If you're new to laptop music, and perhaps to computer music in general, there's no need to be constricted by the software methods of the past – there are new and interesting ways of doing things.

Attitude

The attitude thing is about flexibility, portability, creativity, sociability, and jamming (ran out of suitable 'ity' words!). It's about improvising – in the practical and musi-cal senses of the word; not getting tangled in boundaries and the 'right' way to do things.

Definitely the only way to travel!

Shopping for your laptop

What is this chapter about?

This is where the fun starts – spending your hard-earned on a swanky new laptop, or getting what you need to keep a treasured old machine ticking along for another couple of years.

What you need

A wallet stuffed with cash…how much? Think of a number and double it.

- *I've found that a laptop roughly costs about $1000 more than an equivalently-powered desktop computer. So it's more expensive than a desktop. But it's cheaper than comparable rack synths.* David Das

- *If anything, laptops seem to be diametrically opposed to being used for economic reasons. True it is cheaper to have a laptop than tons of effects boxes and synthesisers, but as far as computer technology goes they still have a long way to come down in price.*

  I remember reading an interview with Aphex Twin who was talking about how laptop music and electronic music is becoming folk music because anybody can use them and travel anywhere with them. The problem with this is that folk music belongs to the people, not some of the people but all the people. You can pick up a guitar at a car-boot sale for £10 , but your average decent laptop is about £1000. I don't believe you can classify anything as folk music until it is fully accessible to everybody. I don't think 'Folk Music For the Financially Secure' has been classified as a genre yet. Ergo Phizmiz.

What makes a music-ready laptop?

Before you buy, you need to know what you want: most laptops available these days have some sort of 'multimedia readiness' … it's pretty much accepted that everybody will be doing something with their computer that includes sound or video somewhere along the way. It's a combination of hardware and OS features … but some computers are still more 'ready' than others.

Like everything else, system requirements depend. They depend on what computer you have, and they depend on what kind of musical use you want to put it

If the choice is between a portable tool and a slightly better non-portable tool, get the portable. You, as a musician will grow and benefit the most when you can go places and write, play and perform with other musos. I really enjoy packing up my little rig, going to someone's house for a day and making new music. SongCarver (performer)

Got myself a decent laptop backpack recently. Am planning to buy better headphones soon. The expenses are never-ending. Lionel Valdellon (performer)

to...somebody who 'only' listens to MP3s and does a little loop-based programming on the side needs different things than somebody who wants to jam on stage with tons of samplers and plug-ins and a controller keyboard attached, and different things from somebody who wants his/her laptop to be at the core of a heavy duty ProTools set-up.

I'll talk later about what to do if you already have a laptop that you want to make music with...this is what you should be looking for if you're buying a new one. As long as your laptop has these hardware features (or most of them), and some basic software, then you can do laptop music!

- *Plenty of RAM and hard disk space, and FireWire. I've found USB audio to be problematic. FireWire is pretty much essential, but it's cheap to add.* David Das

- *Must be fast and quiet.* Thomas Neuhaus (performer)

- *Loads of RAM, large hard disk drive. Fast processor.* Lionel Valdellon

- *PCMCIA slot, FireWire, USB2, large screen, at least 512MB of RAM (and expandable to 1GB), large and fast hard drive (even though it's best to use an external drive with a laptop for speed reasons).* JDG (performer)

- *A good soundcard with line-in and line-out, a decent processor, 256 MB RAM, a hard drive of at least 30GB. And that' s basically it.* Ergo Phizmiz

- *Good memory, good software-based synth, good compatibility with a range of outputs for various devices.* Emilia Telese (artist)

Hard drive

Of course your laptop has to have a hard drive – but not all drives are created equal. First there's the size issue; 1GB used to be a lot, but nowadays you need a rock bottom minimum of 10GB for your drive. A lot of this space will be taken up with software, and any banks of samples that you need regular access to...20GB is

10 GB minimum for your hard drive

acceptable, 40GB is better, 60GB is good. Drive speed concerns some people – multimedia-friendly desktop drives will run at speeds up to 7200rpm; with a laptop you're more likely to encounter speeds of around 4800rpm. Although the speed issue is critical for video production, these 'slower' drives work perfectly well for most music uses.

mindlobster – with 'ceremonial headgear'.

- *There are times when I still use a 466MHz iBook with 320MB of RAM, and certainly with the Mac it seems more important to have RAM than higher MHz numbers; maybe that's a universal thing. Disk speeds? People say that 7200rpm drives are necessary for audio, but you don't really get those in laptops. If you're trying to do a Pro Tools type thing and recording eight tracks at once, you do need a really fast drive, but if you're just doing stereo or even mono in short chunks which is what I tend to do, then the standard drives you get on PowerBooks and iBooks are just fine.* mindlobster (performer).

A gigabyte

Just because you buy a computer with a 10GB drive doesn't mean you will get 10GB of available space; it always shows as less. If you have a 5GB Mac, it will tell you there's 4.7GB available. A 10GB Mac will show you about 9.36GB. There's a lot of industry jiggery pokery about measuring disk space – it all depends on how many bytes you believe make a megabyte...fascinating! Some people feel like they've been cheated when they notice this. My advice...don't worry about it.

CDR drive

A CD drive is essential – if nothing else you'll need it for software installation. CDRW is better because then you can write your own data and audio CDs without an external burner. Those little laptops that come with 'add-on' CD drives should be banned – you end up carrying the CD drive everywhere anyway, 'just in case' you need it to install some software or play a CD, or copy something, so in the end it makes for an even bulkier set-up than an all-in-one. Annoying.

As yet, DVD drives aren't essential for music software installation, though the time is coming fast. There are already software packages that spread their content over four or more CDRs, and people like PowerFX are selling DVDs of audio sample content...so a CDRW/DVD drive is preferable – this will let you play and burn CDs, and play DVDs. Even better (and yet more expensive) is a CDRW/DVDR drive, which will play and burn both CDs and DVDs. You should go the whole hog if you can afford it; it will give you the means to compose, perform and distribute your music and videos from the same laptop.

Battery

Another *of course* item. It's a difficult one to pull off, but if at all possible you should try to get an estimate of battery life before you buy. A laptop that gives less than two hours of battery life isn't worth buying. It's near-impossible to get accurate or relevant real-world comparisons, because manufacturers inevitably err on the optimistic side of things, and no two computer users do the same things for the same amount of time, but even claimed times can give you some indication. Some com-

Quote

If you can burn CDs from your laptop that's an advantage, that's one less piece of outboard gear you need. There are people out there who do gigs, and at the end of the gig you can buy a CD of what they just did; they're burning CDs as they go along. mindlobster (performer).

puters will let you swap batteries without shutting down, simply put it to sleep and flip it over – this is great; a computer with two batteries will give you a whole day's unplugged work…as long as you remembered to charge them the night before!

RAM

Check to see how much memory your laptop can be expanded to hold, then buy as much as you can afford! It's all worth it, RAM is the most important purchase you can make – it will add speed and stability to your computer, whatever OS you're using, and will enable you to run more applications or more plug-ins at once…if you can afford it, buy it at the same time as your computer and get the dealer to install it. Otherwise buy it later and install yourself, it's usually a straight-forward procedure – if you've got little Japanese-style fingers! I haven't, so try as I might, I always end up asking a girl to help me. Oh, the shame…

Soundcard

This isn't like with desktop PC soundcards. Laptop soundcards are not remov-able/upgradeable, and boy, you should be glad of that – desktop Macs are rea-sonably self-contained entities too, but desktop PC users are confronted by a night-marish array of options, with a matching number of potential problems and con-flicts. For the laptop musician, this is more about ensuring that your chosen machine has decent basic sound quality. Any other alterations/improvements to sound quality will revolve around adding external audio interfaces, we'll get to that later.

Screen

Choosing the display size is one of the most important decisions you will make – you're gonna spend a lot of time staring at it. Money comes into it, naturally – the bigger the screen, the more expensive the laptop – but let's put economics aside for a minute. There's no clear-cut right or wrong screen size; a big display, such as the 17 inch on Apple's PowerBook, gives a vast viewing area, which is great for those times when you have two or more apps open at once, or are dealing with horizontal/timeline based tasks, such as sequencing or video editing. However, these big portables are far from compact, and sometimes don't even seem truly 'portable' – they are BIG.

If you want a computer that's easy to move from one location to another, fine, but if you want a computer that'll let you work spontaneously along the way, in tight spots, such as on the train, bus, tube, or in an economy plane cabin on the way to Zurich with no food (for example), then smaller is definitely better.

PC card

These cards (sometimes called PCMCIA or Cardbus) seem almost archaic now, they've been around so long (since the early 1990s), but it's significant that a company like Apple, usually over keen if anything to discard the old ways, retains the format on their 'professional' 15 inch and 17 inch PowerBooks. The audio goodies that use this little slot are high-end items: Digigram's VX Pocket (www.digi-gram.com), Echo's Layla Laptop (www.echoaudio.com), and RME's Hammerfall (www.rme-audio.com). The most affordable PC card option that I'm aware of is Echo's groovy Indigo.

FireWire port

FireWire (or IEEE1394) is a far superior way of doing things than USB (USB1, at any rate) – it's faster, and that higher bandwidth makes it very stable and reliable for audio use. It's used for things like capturing digital video from camcorders – so if it can handle that amount of information, it can easily deal with a little bit of music squeezing through. You might use a setup like a MIDI controller on your USB port, and an audio interface or hard drive on your FireWire port. FireWire devices can also be daisy-chained, that is, you could have a chain that goes: computer – hard drive – DVD burner. According to the FireWire standard, up to 63(!) devices can be chained, but this isn't generally advisable when working with audio – in bandwidth terms, you should leave as much room as possible for your music to get through. Chaining bus-powered devices is particularly inadvisable. A new faster version of FireWire is now appearing – see below.

USB port

Universal Serial Bus. A relatively recent arrival to the connectivity scene, this is what all modern computers use to connect printers, mice, joysticks, scanners, hubs, graphics tablets, etc. For us laptop musicians, USB is what we use to connect MIDI keyboards, MIDI controllers, some audio interfaces, and most importantly, USB lights and fans! USB2 is becoming more common, enabling faster connection speeds.

Two USB ports are ideal – it might save you using a USB hub later once you add more gadgets – and not all USB peripherals like working with hubs. On stage I use one port for a MIDI controller, and one for a light. USB can also be useful for connecting 3.5 inch floppy disk drives – a lot of musicians who are migrating from using hardware sequencers have an archive of material on floppy disk. Maybe it should be possible to rent floppy drives when needed, because for a lot of migrating musos, this is a once-only job!

Speed

Things used to be pretty clear-cut when it was just FireWire and USB. Now there's USB2 and FireWire 800 to confuse things. Here's the relative data-transfer speeds (sourced from www.apple.com):

```
            USB1.1 = 12MBPS
            USB2.0 = 480MBPS
FireWire 400 (IEEE1394) = 400MBPS
FireWire 800 (IEEE1394b) = 800MBPS
```

Hope that clears it up. You can expect USB1-compatible audio/MIDI devices to gradually disappear, in the face of the speedier opposition. The sooner the better, I say.

Headphone socket

- *Any off-the-shelf laptop should be able to make some musical noise, but it needs to have very good quality stereo out, whether that's built in the laptop or you have to buy an external device to help you get that. I don't think you should buy a laptop that doesn't have good sound as standard because they're so often used for multimedia now. Even if you're just going to watch DVDs on it you don't want rubbish sound coming out.* mindlobster

Otherwise known as a stereo out, always in the form of a 3.5mm mini jack socket. This is likely to be your most regular point of audio contact with your laptop. Also vital for connecting your laptop to external amplification (unless you have some sort of USB/FireWire/PC card interface). If you want to stick to using this connection, make sure the output is noise-free, otherwise you'll be forced to buy an interface anyway – anybody who uses an early Apple iBook (like the orange ones) will know what I'm talking about!

You shouldn't take anything for granted. If possible, listen to the laptop's output before you buy, on headphones and/or speakers; sometimes even two instances of the same model will sound different due to variations in manufacturing tolerances. Ask around, hear what other users say about their computers. I firmly believe that Apple computers still lead the way with off-the-shelf sound quality – sound engineers are always happy to meet you if you've got a PowerBook!

Speakers

You may plan to spend most of your laptop music time connected to headphones, or an amplifier, or a PA, but there are times when it's handy to use your laptop's built-in speakers. Don't expect too much from them though; they are pretty small after all, and you'll experience a distinct lack of bass. Using these speakers is NOT about getting a quality listening experience, it's just a convenient way of hearing some kind of noise from your laptop, that's all. *Never* I repeat *never* try to mix using the speakers on your laptop!

Stereo input

Not every laptop has one, but they can be useful if you want to connect your laptop to a microphone, or a pre-amp, or a cassette deck, or a turntable...and you don't want to (or can't afford to) use a USB or FireWire interface. For a lot of users, a computer with a stereo input and output, as long as they're relatively clean, is all the audio connections they'll ever need, but remember, microphones need to go through an external pre-amp before their signal enters your computer.

Built-in microphone

- *My main mic now is the built-in mic on the PowerBook. I've got songs where I've sung vocals into the PowerBook and just ended up keeping those for the final mix.* mindlobster

Most but not all laptops come with one of these, sometimes manifested as a tiny hole visible in the display's surround, or, in the case of Titanium G4 PowerBooks, concealed inside the left speaker grill. These microphones are of low quality, and they excel at picking up the noise of your computer, *but you should use them anyway* – sometimes a low quality microphone is a beautiful thing – they are very useful for grabbing demo vocals on those times when inspiration strikes (it's got to happen one day), and can be great for gathering semi-random location/ambient sounds. Not as good or as controllable or as 'professional' as a minidisc recorder, perhaps, but recordings made with laptop microphones have a special charm all of their own, and the immediacy is unbeatable.

Fun with built-in mics

All you need is a built-in mic and Ableton Live, and the world is yours to plunder (sonically speaking). Public spaces are ideal – coffee shops, museums, parks, wherever. Built-in mics are great for capturing voices and machine sounds – coffee machines, cups or plates hitting the table. Launch Live, then start recording and minimise the application so it isn't visible on screen. Get a text document or a graphic file or something on screen; nobody will know you're recording, nobody will hassle you (this isn't about sneakily recording individuals without their knowledge – well it is actually, but not in a harmful way, they won't be recognisable at the end, they're just source material for your audio creation). Just remember that if you do any typing, or talk or clear your throat or call your friend, that will be recorded too – but that can be part of the fun. Live is the perfect tool for manipulating sounds collected this way – turning them into ambient loops, rhythmic parts, or even 'lead' parts, and then mixing them with more traditional sounds such as beats or vocals. Psychoacoustic music – hey, it's supposed to sound like washing machines!

Choose your OS: Windows vs Mac vs Linux

You can define laptops in many ways – by their appearance, their features, their size, or by which glowing little fruit they have on their lid. But it's the operating system which you have to deal with on a daily basis; that's what will define your experience...

For most people, choosing an OS is the same as choosing a computer. They come together, and users don't switch platforms midstream unless they have a very good reason. For many, it's an arbitrary decision based on what's used in the office, or what's available at a good price in the local computer store – and the truth is that people quickly get used to whatever they have in front of them day to day.

We all know about the dumb arguments people get into about the superiority of Windows over Mac or vice versa; 'my platform is tuffer than yours' – they take it so seriously, there's a lot of needless vitriol. The truth is that those arguments matter less now than ever before – there's no need to bash Steve Jobs or Bill Gates. Most good audio applications are available for Windows and Mac, and both OS's are going strong, working at very high levels. Wherever possible, I've covered material which will be relevant to users of both Windows and Mac based computers. Furthermore, if there's any Linux options, I'll try to let you know about those too; I'm very fair. The playing field is levelling out; it's the apps that you use and how well you use them that matter. Platform-related issues will be kept to a minimum – I won't be explaining the ins and outs of installations and configurations for various operating systems.

Below are some of the reasons why people choose a particular OS. All I can say about this is be open minded, don't get too hung up on stupid 'Mac is better than Windows is better than Linux' wars...make some music instead!

Why use Windows XP?

There are a lot of good reasons for musicians to consider Windows XP:

- It's the best incarnation of Windows so far, in terms of features and performance.
- The world's most popular OS – which means there is a lot of software available – some of it even legal.
- Popularity = compatibility.
- It runs on cheap computers.
- It's as close as you're gonna get to Mac OSX on a PC.

- *XP is the standard these days. if you're going to buy a Dell or Vaio you're going to get XP. XP is a lot faster than earlier versions of Windows, and the environment is nice. People will get that because the vast amount of software – games, music, you name it – comes out for XP. The computers are cheaper too. Most people learn how to use Windows at school – everybody buys it because everybody else has it. IriXx (musician/writer)*

Windows XP – the best incarnation of
Windows so far.

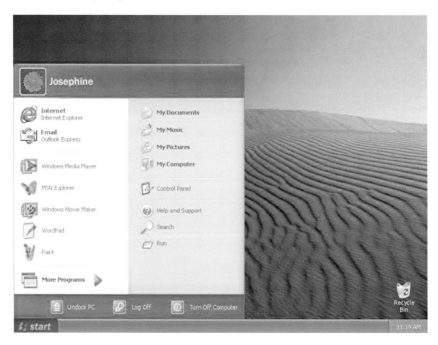

Why use Mac OSX?

There are a lot of good reasons for musicians to consider Mac OSX:

- Mac OSX is running at a high level now. I pulled OS9 from my computers in May 2003 – it's going to be totally extinct very soon.
- It's the OS for people who don't want to tinker with their computer – which means you can spend more time on your music.
- Core Audio/Core MIDI. Audio and MIDI tasks are now handled within the OS, negating the requirement for third party utilities such as the dreaded OMS. It's now much easier to get audio and MIDI apps talking to each other on a Mac.
- An increasing number of music apps are available, including more free and cheap ones than ever before, on the Mac platform.
- The integration between Apple's notorious 'iApps' – iTunes, iMovie, iDVD, iDisk, etc. You might think the 'i' thing is funny, but it *works*.
- You can use a PowerBook – the best reason of all.

Mac OSX – goodbye to OMS!

I have to admit I'm biased in this regard, I use OSX all the time. You can be more confident that the sound quality will be there straight away, and Apple are more upfront about pushing their audio features these days, with iTunes, ITMS, the iPod, the optical audio connections on the desktop G5s – there's still a pro studio vibe to using a Macintosh.

There are also considerable support benefits in machine and OS coming from the same source. There are times when you're running Ableton Live on the Mac and everything starts working together, and it begins to feel almost like running one of the old hardware grooveboxes. It's very easy to get the audio and MIDI apps working together. There's nothing like the Apple level of integration on other platforms – I'm told that Windows people are intensely jealous of it.

Why use Linux?

There are a lot of good reasons for musicians to consider Linux:

- Those attracted to Linux have the most choice when it comes to hardware – it will run on a Mac or a PC.
- Linux is based on open-source code – software can be copied and shared freely (though the exact details can get more complicated). Using Linux makes a statement about copyright and ownership.
- Linux is good if you like to tinker at a very deep level. That should make it diametrically opposed to the Mac OS, but Linux and Mac users do seem to unite against the common Microsoft foe.
- There are Linux apps which sound unlike anything for Mac OSX or Windows XP.
- Linux has a promising future as a music platform, especially considering its highly tweakable structure – it's the easiest OS to optimise for a single purpose.

Linux – will run on a Mac or a PC.

For the Linux newbie, the worst thing to deal with is the overabundance of versions of the OS itself; all offering a particular combination of features and political posture. Debian, Red Hat, Gentoo, and Slackware are all Linux configurations (IriXx recommends Mandrake 9.2 for newbies).

Linux

I assume that you're at least partially familiar with Windows and Mac OS (currently in XP and OSX versions respectively). You might not know about Linux, an open-source OS – or rather a range of OS's – started by Linus Torvalds in 1991. Linux has become the system of choice for users concerned about issues of copyright and ownership of software. If you're interested in this you should start your investigation at www.linux.org.

Linux can be installed on a PC or Mac – you can install it alongside or instead of the original OS. It's even possible to buy certain laptops with Linux pre-installed, with or without Windows.

Linux has its own collection of music apps – some of them are similar to more mainstream apps, others are more distinctive. Linux will work with several different audio formats including AIF and WAV, but the format mostly closely associated with Linux is Ogg Vorbis, a means of compression similar to MP3, but claimed to have superior sound quality, and without the licensing requirements (the MP3 format is owned by the Fraunhofer Institute). The list of applications features DJ tools, drum machines, signal processors, synths, vocoders, sequencers, multitrack recorders, and even guitar tuners. Jack is the Linux equivalent of Apple's Coreaudio, and most recent versions of Linux music apps are 'Jackified'. For plug-ins you can use the LADSPA format, which apparently now hosts VSTs too.

The thing that makes Linux most interesting to laptop musicians is its low demand on the computer's resources. An older computer which would struggle to run OSX or XP (if at all) can serve as a home for some of the distinctive Linux sounds. If you own a computer with limited resources or are lucky enough to have a second one just laying around, Linux could give it a new lease of life.

- *Linux by nature has a very low demand on the CPU – you can use very low spec computers. I know somebody who produces quite nice music on a Pentium 166 with something ridiculous like 32 megs of RAM. It's ideal if you've got an old laptop knocking around.* IriXx

- *I'm a Mac user, using OSX. I'd use anything…if a Linux developer came out with something better than Ableton Live I'd use that. I don't think people should be dogmatic about that. I've used little battery powered sequencers – you use what's available. It's nice to lust after gear but you should always be looking at making the most out of what you've already got instead of spending all your time dreaming, you shouldn't blame your equipment and say 'I would be a good musician if I had a PowerBook instead of an iBook, or if I had a Sony instead of a Dell or whatever ', you should be saying 'I can be good now'.* mindlobster

Choose your own OS – don't blame me!
But know this – I am, and always will be, a Mac user.

Examples of current laptops

It's good and necessary to conduct some research before you spend your money. Laptops (like all computers) have their peculiarities, limitations, and bad habits – the drive's too small, the flap covering the ports snaps off, the rubber parts disintegrate, it gets too hot and burns your legs...there's always going to be something that isn't quite right. *But* you can go too far, you can get too clever – you can get so over-informed that you spend more money than you can really afford, or nothing seems good enough and you keep waiting for the next model that is 'just around the corner', and end up not buying anything.

What fun is that?

If there's a model available now, that does what you want and fits your budget, buy it, then stop looking at the new computers.

It would be futile to attempt to list specific models of laptop, and compare their features; the list would be ancient history before it saw print. It is possible and reasonable however to look at some current models as examples of what's around, just to give you some ideas.

Quote

*D*on't buy cheap gear. It will only bite you in the end. JDG

Apple iBook G4 12 inch Combo Drive

This is currently Apple's base model portable, very widespread in education – a semi-stylish workhorse. Get more details from www.apple.com.

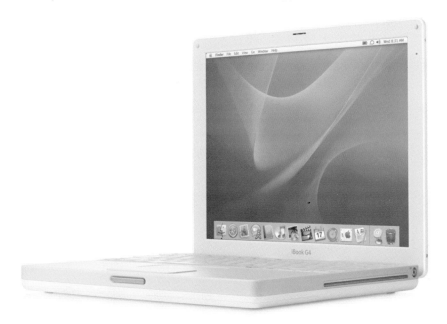

OS	Mac OSX
Screen size	12 inch
Resolution	1024 x 768
Weight	2.2kg
Processor	800MHz
Hard drive	30GB
RAM maximum	640MB
Optical drive	DVDR/CDRW Combo Drive
Ports	FireWire (1), USB2 (2), Modem/Airport Extreme ready/Bluetooth adaptor optional
	VGA, s-video, composite video out
	Stereo speakers
	Headphone out
Internal microphone	
Battery life	Up to 6 hours

Sony Vaio **TR1MP**

This is just one of Sony's ever-changing Vaio range...sweet. The integrated camera is a nice touch. More info at www.sony.com.

OS	Windows XP Professional Edition
Screen size	10.6 inch
Resolution	1280 x 768
Weight	1.41kg
Processor	900MHz
Hard drive	30GB
RAM maximum	1GB
Optical drive	DVDR/CDRW Combo Drive
Memory stick storage	
Ports	FireWire (1), USB2 (2), Modem/Blue tooth/wireless LAN
	VGA video out
	Stereo speakers
	Headphone out
Internal microphone	
Battery life	Up to 3.5 hours

Compaq Tablet PC TC1000

There's no sign as yet that tablet-style PCs will catch on, never mind find a musical use, but I think there's potential. Has anybody out there tried one of these with an audio editor, or Ableton Live? More info from www.compaq.com.

OS	Windows XP Tablet Edition
Screen size	10.4 inch
Resolution	1024 x 768
Weight	1.34kg
Processor	1GHz
Hard drive	30GB
RAM maximum	512MB
External docking station, removable keyboard, pen input	
Compact flash slot	
Ports	USB (2)
	Modem
	VGA video out
	Stereo speakers
	Headphone out
Internal microphone	
Battery life	Up to 5 hours

Build to order options from music dealers

The music is allowed to be complicated if that's what floats your boat, but there's no need for unnecessary suffering when it comes to choosing and setting up your computer. There are two ways to keep this process simple:

1   Buy a Mac

or

2   Buy a preconfigured Windows-based laptop from a music dealer. This is becoming more common these days, and is highly recommended if you just want to get down to the music stuff with the minimum of mess. A system that has been configured, tested and is guaranteed to work, is about as good as it's going to get in this uncertain world.

Millennium Music (www.millennium-music.biz)

Currently have around a dozen laptop packages available to order on their site, which include assorted selections of music software and interfaces. As if that wasn't enough choice, you can add any extras you might want, or you can call them and discuss even more options.

Red Submarine (www.sub.co.uk)

Offer a similar service. Visit their website, and almost every aspect of the computer can be made to measure, again with a wide choice of add-ons.

There's got to be a lot of tinker time saved with these deals – it arrives at your home or studio ready to rock, and you get the security of knowing if it goes wrong, you can take it to somebody who will understand the software and hardware that's involved. However, I don't think this is an ideal solution for everyone – if you're running a computer that you didn't set up yourself, every little thing that goes wrong (and things will go wrong, be sure of that), will be an unknown. You're either going to have to return the laptop to your dealer every time it has a problem, or learn how to fix them yourself anyway. Just because it comes all set-up and ready to go doesn't mean it's going to be as reliable as a groovebox or drum machine.

The other issue I have with these is harder to pin down, and could seem a little bit unfair. Computers bought like this don't have any character; they are faceless efficient machines, which is good if you're a 'techie' type, but the lack of idiosyncrasies makes using them seem kind of flat. Well, I guess that can be fixed...if you get one of these then make sure you install something strange on it ASAP and cover the lid in stickers, then it will truly be yours!

Is that old laptop up to it?

• *You can use just about anything. I'm fond of using retro gear but you've got to accept the limitations if you use low spec machines. I would say, having moved to a 650MHz Pentium 3 machine, this is the first time I've been able to run Ableton Live and improvise on stage with no crashes!* IriXx

iBooks, Vaios, Tablets, pre-packaged music laptops, that's all great. But maybe you haven't got enough cash for a new laptop – although they're far more accessible now than they were a few years ago, buying a laptop still entails handing over a big heap of cash, and they're always more expensive than their desktop counterparts.

What you gonna do?

One path to affordable notebook nirvana is end-of-line discounts. If you can tolerate buying a slightly less than state-of-the-art machine, dealers often want to clear stock of old models just as new ones are announced or released. There are a lot of places to look for this kind of thing, but (strange though it might sound) you should try the John Lewis chain of department stores (www.johnlewis.com). They have good discounts on end-of-line and ex-demo computers, and offer their own one year guarantee in addition to the manufacturer's warranty. Furthermore, they are Mac and PC dealers, so you can see a wide range of computers from both platforms; just don't expect any in-depth technical knowledge from the staff.

Buying second-hand is another alternative, but you have to be careful. I've bought used computers in the past, and so far (touch wood) I've been lucky – I've paid low prices and got very well-kept laptops – but not everybody has the same experience.

- *Have I ever bought a used laptop? Yes, and now it doesn't work too well anymore!* Ergo Phizmiz

There are things you can do to minimise the risks. Make sure the computer has the original disks and documentation. Inspect the casing for damage. Check the screen for marks. Run it for a while on mains power, and then battery power. Listen to the computer – is it making any odd noises? Check it has the advertised amount of RAM in it. Put in a CD and play some songs, listen to them on speakers and head-phones. Does the computer has an onboard microphone? If so, test it. If you've got any handy, try to connect some peripherals and make sure they work as intended. Has the seller got a case for it? A laptop that's lived in a case or bag is a safer bet than one that's been knocking around unprotected. Look at the owner – try to read their minds, because that might be what it comes down to. And that reminds me – I would *strongly* discourage buying a computer from an auction website, or in any other situation where you can't check it out first. It's one thing to use the internet to find for-sale laptops in the first place, that's great, but don't buy if you can't try!

- *Laptops, by their very nature, are portable and are frequently carried around. If you buy one used – whether off eBay or from someone you know – you have no way of knowing exactly how well it's been treated, or how many times it's been dropped. I have a friend with a laptop who is an absolute klutz. His laptop has been repaired more times than I can count. Yet it looks nearly new.* David Das

- *I've bought second-hand, that's all I could afford. If you're gonna buy second-hand take an expert along, see if it's been abused. Ex-demo, ex-lease models are good, mine I bought from an Apple reseller. It had been leased to an architectural company, so it had been nicely looked after by respectable professionals!* J-Lab

And...please don't buy stolen computers. Not only are you participating in the theft of somebody else's beloved laptop, you're going to get pretty underwhelming technical support. Clue – if it's being sold to you in a pub car park, then chances are it's hot.

But maybe you already have an old laptop, perhaps one that you used to use for work/college, knocking around, or stashed in the cupboard under the stairs, one that seems too old to use for anything so 'modern' as music creation. Well, it may not be the fastest or lightest or best-specified thing around, but you might be able to use it for some kind of music.

Older or lower spec laptops can still be fun – if you're willing to accept their lim-itations, a little housework and judicious upgrading can work wonders. Going back further, there may be some more primitive laptops that also have potential. With those you run into different problems – they may lack CD drives; they may have very low disk and memory capacities; they may be very slow; they can create tim-ing problems. Some of these problems can be solved, others can't. Connectivity, for instance, can be a real problem, as new computer audio interfaces require USB or FireWire ports.

The most important thing to stress is the need to be flexible. If you're really fixated on running a particular application or connecting a certain piece of hardware, this might not work for you. Using an older laptop can be a chance to experiment – the older they get, the more you have to experiment!

If you are using a more recent but low spec laptop, with USB, maybe no FireWire, and with limited disk space, memory, and MHz, then most of your problems are about housekeeping and resource management.

Begin by checking the manufacturer's website for information about the laptop – what type of memory does it use, and how much can be added? Are there any relevant downloadable firmware/software updates? Is the hard drive or the floppy/optical drive upgradeable? Make sure you have the latest possible version of your chosen OS installed, along with drivers for any peripherals you have. If you're going to use it only for music, remove all unwanted apps and files – strip it down!

Connect it to some speakers and/or headphones and play a CD or some audio files from CDR. Is the sound quality OK? If not, then you will have to buy an audio interface, or settle for using the laptop to drive external hardware via MIDI.

There are a lot of resource-saving techniques to apply once you're up and running, they make a huge amount of difference. Make sure your computer isn't running any other apps in the background – give it less things to do at once. Disable networking and file indexing features, as well as any antivirus/crash protection applications (remember to turn 'em all back on afterwards!).

Keep your number of tracks down. Avoid using plug-ins that require a lot of juice, and don't run too many at once. If you are using a lot of effects, and you don't need real-time control over their parameters, you can mix the relevant song sections to disk as stereo or mono files and reimport them. Record in mono if stereo isn't necessary. Experiment with lower sample rates (ltrading off between ower sound quality and smaller files) on non-critical sounds – the difference may not be heard in the mix (especially live), and, strangely, some sounds are 'better' when downsampled in this way.

There's a limit to how far it's worth going with hardware updates to ageing laptops. Upgrade options are fewer anyway, and more costly than for desktops – on desktops almost everything is replaceable, but it's not so economically viable to keep old laptops going. Upgrades are possible, to hard drives and occasionally even CPUs, but it's really not worth getting into this unless you've got a profound emotional attachment to your laptop, or you expect to keep it for a long time.

Two of the most important things you need for laptop music are USB and FireWire ports – they are essential for connecting modern audio and MIDI peripherals. Otherwise you're plunged back into the dark ages of SCSI and modem ports – you don't want to go there. If your laptop has a PC Card slot (many do), then you can insert a third party card which will add the missing ports, giving you access to all the latest interfaces. There are a few of these cards around, most adding a single FireWire or USB port, although Macally (www.macally.com) have a card which adds two USB1 ports, and Orange Micro's OrangeCombo adds two FireWire ports (1x 6-pin, 1x4-pin) AND two USB2.0 ports – very handy. One of these cards might be the best buy you make, giving you access to all that FireWire fun (www.orangemicro.com)!

Get into good habits with Ableton Live

Ableton Live (www.ableton.com) is such a popular application with laptop users, it serves as a good example to illustrate some resource-saving techniques. Most of the above suggestions apply. Keep the number of tracks down and avoid overuse of effects (especially that greedy reverb). Render and re-import or bounce effects-heavy sections. If you've used the loop tool in the sample display to select a certain portion of a sample, and you're sure you don't want the rest of it, then open your audio editor and ditch the unwanted chunks – a lot of disk space and a lot of RAM can be saved this way. Like many other apps, Live can save a self-contained set which copies all clips referred to in the set to a new folder – this is another good way of managing disk space.

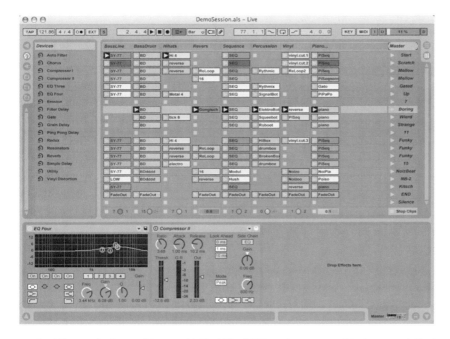

Ableton Live – you'll be seeing more of this later!

And if you don't need it to add FireWire/USB ports, you could always put that PC Card slot to other use by adding a PC Card-based audio interface, like those from RME or Echo...more on these later!

As laptops age, their original batteries will deteriorate, giving shorter operating times. You should contact the manufacturer's website to check the availability of replacements, and there are third party replacement laptop batteries around, claiming to give improved life...start with Newer Technology (www.newertech.com).

Orange Micro Combo – USB and FireWire.

Software for old laptops

Even if you get the hardware side sorted out, the software side of things can be difficult. You'll have to find apps that work on whatever is the latest OS you can install – this is where Linux users can have an advantage.

• *I don't use any illegal software. I use only GNU GPL software to make my music; no pirated copies of Reason here. To me commercial software is now irrelevant, with Suse Linux 8.2 now I get everything I need, and 9.0 looks even better, with the new 2.6 kernel the system latency will be even lower, so I can*

get more complex with TerminatorX, like being able to trigger samples from the MIIDI sequencer and sync them to my MIDI controller guitar processor to have my guitar effects synced to TerminatorX for even more mind bending fun.'
Brian Redfern (DJ/musician)

Overclocking – or how to destroy a perfectly good computer

Overclocking is the term for resetting your computer to increase processor speed. This can work successfully on desktop computers, if you know what you're doing, but it's a real warranty buster. It will drastically increase the temperature of the computer... on a desktop you can fit a more powerful fan, but there's no room for that on a laptop. *Avoid*.

There's also an increasing number of apps which won't recognise screen resolutions below 1024 x 768. I ran into this when trying to run a recent Native Instruments app on an old 'clamshell' iBook. I was trying a demo version...and was glad I hadn't paid for the app before discovering the incompatibility.

- *If it's a hassle to use, don't buy it. you won't use it anyway.* SongCarver

Keep it as minimal as you can...there is less to go wrong...don't get railroaded into buying add-ons that you don't really need...sure it's fun to have lots of new toys, I enjoy that too, but laptop music is about portability; the idea is to keep your rig simple and portable – otherwise you will get tired of humping it all around.

And maybe you don't need to update or upgrade at all, maybe your laptop's fine as it is. If it's working well, and doing everything you want, if it's reliable and letting you simply get on with the work, then leave it alone!

- *I do think there's a big point – if it ain't broke don't fix it. I'd been using Windows 98 until I got my new laptop with XP installed. Generally I only upgrade if it has features that I need.* IriXx

- *I'm not interested in all the computer nitty-gritty that people often get caught up in. To be honest I've no idea what many computer terms mean. I know how to turn it on and use the software, and know what I need to know to be able to do what I want to do. And that's enough for me.* Ergo Phizmiz

Use what you have, make the most of it, don't waste your time dreaming about that 'ultimate' system you saw in a movie thanks to a product placement deal based on cash rather than merit. While you're waiting to afford the 17' PowerBook/23' Cinema Display combo, dust off that Compaq or Dell or old PowerBook 3400 that's in the cupboard, and use it – run it into the ground.

- *I'm still running Mac OS9, so I've got as far as I'm ever gonna get with that. If something comes along and offers a significant performance then I'll go for that, but I'm not an upgrade fetishist.* J-Lab

People think Steve Jobs and Bill Gates owe them something ... they don't. You buy the product and you owe them nothing, and they owe you some technical support, and that's it. If you are lucky enough to be shopping for a new laptop, choose the best one for what you do – don't worry about the labels.

Listening to laptop music

Why use a laptop to listen to music at home?

Whatever purpose you bought your laptop for, it can do double duty as a CD deck and MP3 player. AND it'll let you do things you couldn't with a regular CD player, like add groovy visuals that respond to the music, browse for and buy new music online, create and manage playlists, and of course – controversially – share MP3s and copy CDs. Throw in the laptop's built-in speakers and headphone socket, and you've got a self-contained music system.

Yes you can do all of this with a desktop computer too, and it would be pretty extravagant to buy a laptop solely for playing CDs, but the point is, if you already own one, listening to and organising music is a piece of cake for your laptop. And there's always the laptop's standard advantages of portability – easy to move from room to room, and a very small footprint – it doesn't take up much space, and it packs down nice and tidy.

Software for your listening pleasure – iTunes (www.apple.com)

If you've bought a laptop that will play CDs (that must be all of them these days), it'll include some sort of CD player software. What player you get depends on your OS of choice – there have been many knocking around in the past, such as WinAmp and MacAmp (can you guess which platforms they were for?), but these days it's broadly true to say that Windows users get the Windows Media Player, Mac users get iTunes, and Linux users have XMMS.

Furthermore, with the availability of Apple's iTunes for Mac and Windows, I suggest that you cease your search for playback/encoding software now.

iTunes is one of Apple's notorious iApps, an integral part of their 'digital hub' lifestyle concept. That may or may not attract you, but if you look beyond the marketing, it's a very useful and well-developed means of listening to music on your computer. And sweetest of all, iTunes is free – if you haven't got it yet, download it from Apple's website at www.apple.com (Mac OSX, Windows 2000 or Windows XP required).

Apple's iTunes – available for Mac and Windows

Of course, iTunes is more than a mere player. You can copy individual songs or whole CDs to your drive in AAC or MP3 formats, and when you're online you can access the CD database (www.cddb.com) and iTunes will automatically add song, album, and artist information. Songs can be arranged in searchable playlists, including smart playlists which can sort your songs based on conditions such as 'most recently played' or 'most recently added'. Songs within playlists can be shuffled, repeated, or looped.

There are a couple of handy features for when you're listening to your playlists – Sound Check, which automatically evens out all songs to a similar volume level, and Crossfade playback, a semi-DJ style feature which does what it says – as one song nears its end and begins to fade out, the next one fades in. Crossfade times of up to 12 seconds are possible (this can only be applied globally – to all songs).

The song files and playlist info can be kept on your computer if you've got enough disk space, or moved to an external drive, or burned to a standard audio or MP3 CD, or archived to DVD. If you're on a network, you can setup iTunes to 'share' your music with other users; this works on wireless networks between laptops too – I've tried it, just to see if it works, but I haven't found a reason for using it yet!

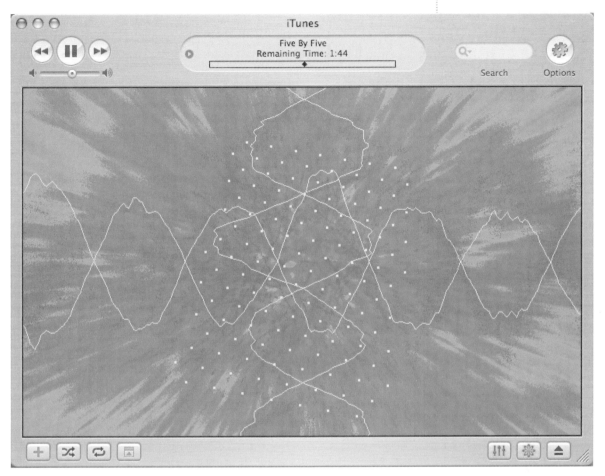

iTunes Visualizer gives a full-screen
abstract/psychedelic accompaniment to your
music.

If you've got nothing better to do, you can settle down to enjoy iTunes' Visualizer, which gives a full-screen abstract/psychedelic accompaniment to your music, with beat-sensitive effects. There are a few user-definable options, accessed by keys 0-9, and you can choose to run the Visualizer in the iTunes window, or at full screen.

But there's more to iTunes, a lot more. If you own an Apple iPod (which also works with Windows) you can transfer your playlists to it via FireWire or USB2, and enjoy listening on the move. Current iPod models contain 10, 20 and 40GB drives, enabling storage of up to 10,000 songs, equalling 4 weeks of uninterrupted music-that should be enough. The iPod is a great invention, and deceptive in its under-stated appearance. It's an extremely versatile unit, which is why it's featured so often in this book.

A development in the iTunes story is the iTunes Music Store (ITMS), an online store accessible from within the iTunes interface itself, where visitors can browse through thousands of songs and audiobooks, hear brief previews, and then download tracks for a reasonable $1 each. Once a song is downloaded, it can be incorporated into iTunes playlists in the same way as any other song, and of course moved to an iPod. ITMS has become massively popular in a short time, although a broadband or other high speed connection is recommended if you intend to download a lot of songs.

iTunes Music Store (ITMS) –
legal downloads can be fun!

Talking of fast connections – if yours is reasonably speedy, or at least consistent, you can use iTunes to enjoy streaming internet radio broadcasts (I like Sleepbot – www.sleepbot.com). Favourite stations can be added to your iTunes library for easy recall at a later date. It's not supposed to be possible to record these broadcasts to your drive from within iTunes, but, ahem, there are ways round these things...

It should also be noted that iTunes can copy CD tracks to AIFF and WAV. This little-advertised fact means that you can make compression-free copies from CDs – also very useful for musicians who want to use iTunes to compile and burn their CDs without any loss in quality.

iTunes comes highly recommended – for Mac AND Windows. Most of the Mac users I've talked to have started using iTunes now, and many of them have taken to using the AAC encoding. It remains to be seen whether iTunes will achieve the same dominance amongst Windows users, but so far it looks promising – the initial response to the Windows release has been positive to say the least.

Audio file formats

- MP3 – the web standard for audio file compression – generally considered an acceptable trade-off between file size and quality. Created by the Fraunhofer Institute (www.iis.fraunhofer.de)
- AAC – more recent format than MP3, sounds better (allegedly) and makes smaller files.
- WAV – default uncompressed audio format for Windows.
- AIFF – default uncompressed audio format for Mac, equivalent to WAV.
- OGG Vorbis – similar in quality to MP3 (claimed to be better), but derived from open source code to avoid license/royalty issues (Fraunhofer require a royalty payment for use of the MP3 format).

Playing CDs

If you're running your laptop from its battery – it uses less power to play songs as MP3s/AACs/etc from the hard drive than it does to spin and play a CD.

iTunes Visualizer

Despite its simplicity, there is some interactivity to be enjoyed with the iTunes Visualizer. Shortcuts can be used to alter the course of the effects – stored in the 0–9 keys, and third party plug-ins are available, adding even more visual effects.

Connecting to stereo speakers

In a way, of course, your laptop *is* a home entertainment system, you don't need to connect it to anything except maybe some headphones. I've spent many happy hours with the laptop perched on my lap (where else?), watching DVDs – or it's on the table, and I'm doing stuff while iTunes is doing its own thing, maybe with some fine full screen visuals to accompany it. Buying some speakers, however, will enhance your listening/viewing experience.

The cheapest and easiest way to do this, assuming of course that you've already got some sort of stereo system, is to treat your laptop like any other piece of hi-fi gear such as a cassette or CD deck, and use a stereo mini jack-to-left/right phono lead to connect it to your amp – most amps have an 'aux' input, use that if it's free. Cables like this are available everywhere, and in good lengths too, so you don't have to leave your laptop teetering on a book on a box on a chair to reach the amp. A set-up like that might be enough for most people – why pay more? Everything after that is about extras.

Audio interface

The next most extravagant candidate for improving your listening experience is a simple audio interface – a small box that will connect to your USB or FireWire port and give you stereo output at a much higher quality than from your headphone socket. This is the laptop equivalent of upgrading the soundcard on a desktop computer.

The Griffin Technology iMic (www.griffintechnology.com) has proven very popular for Mac users, and is about as minimal an interface as you could get, being basically a yo-yo sized object on a very short USB cable, supplying mini jack stereo in and out. The only problem with the iMic is that it's so simple and inscrutable that if you run into problems while using it, it's difficult to tell if the problems emanate from the iMic, the computer, or the software. Having said that, a lot of people seem to get on well with the iMic, so maybe it's just me being stupid...wouldn't be the first time.

Edirol (www.edirol.com) were among the first to latch onto USB audio/MIDI, and they're still dominant in the field, recently adding their first USB2-compatible device to a bulging catalogue. For simple stereo playback, the UA-1A is a good bet. It's as straightforward as it gets – no drivers are required for Mac or PC (there are reportedly Linux drivers in circulation too), simply plug and play. This unit is slightly less basic than the iMic, featuring stereo phono in and out, and a helpful LED to let you know it's alive. I've tested this with a variety of computers and applications, and it's worked fine in my experience – more reliably than the iMic. Other models from Edirol supplement the phono outs with optical digital outs, giving even better sound quality as long as you're connecting them to something with optical ins!

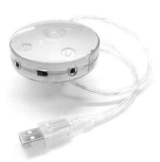

Griffin Technology iMic – basic USB audio interface for Mac.

Edirol UA-1A - USB audio for Mac/Windows.

USB audio – caution

USB audio, though the technology has improved since the early days (ie a couple of years ago), can still be patchy, especially for recording. Many USB audio interfaces are referred to in this book; if you want to buy one, you should endeavour to try it first, or get some assurance that you can obtain a refund if it doesn't work with your system. Some manufacturers have compatibility information on their websites.

There are plenty of other simple USB audio devices on the market, including M-Audio's Transit, which features stereo analogue in/out and digital in/out, and looks really nice (important), and the Sonica (from M-Audio's 'consumer' range), with digital and analogue out only (www.m-audio.com).

M-Audio Transit – it's cute and it's USB!

M-Audio Sonica – M-Audio rule the roost when it comes to laptop-friendly gear.

Some USB audio interfaces have multiple outputs – more than the usual stereo left/right. eMagic's A26 has six outputs (www.emagic.com) and the separated-at-birth (ie they look alike) Maya EX71 and Gigaport have a massive eight outputs each (www.audiotrak.co.uk and www.esi-pro.com). This makes them good candidates for surround sound applications, whether that's mixing surround audio or watching DVDs.

Gigaport – that's a lot of connections for a USB box.

As USB2 and FireWire based interfaces become more common, and hopefully trickle down to the cheaper end of the market, it could be that USB1 based audio interfaces will disappear – this will be a good thing. USB audio has always been about fitting a quart in a pint pot, or whatever that expression is – use it if you must, but it's never gonna be perfect.

Small speaker systems

If you don't have a hi-fi system/don't want one/can't afford one/haven't got room for one, you can always go back to basics and connect some portable 'Walkman'-type speakers to your laptop's headphone output. These speakers inevitably sound nasty, but they are cheap, and very portable, especially if you get battery powered ones. I have a small Philips pair, which actually don't sound too bad. They're great for doing presentations, hotel room listening, and in the studio as 'low end' speakers for comparison with 'better' monitors during mix sessions.

Recently, more credible, more expensive, and better sounding versions of these small speaker systems have become available, applying higher standards of design and sound quality. Harman Kardon's (www.harmankardon.com) SoundSticks and iSub subwoofer are a Mac-only option, again using USB instead of the headphone output. These sound good, and the iSub adds much-needed bass. Of course the looks are equally important with these transparent babies – there's nothing else like them.

JBL's Creatures (www.jbl.com) also target the design-conscious laptop user – though there's no reason why they can't be used with a desktop computer or a Walkman (they use mini jack connection instead of USB), they somehow are always seen with Apple's white iBooks or iPods. This is another three-speaker system, and again aesthetics take priority as the Creatures are available in white, silver, or blue, each with different colour downward firing LEDs to cast a glow over late-night listening activities. Invite your friends over and stumble around in the dark, risking life and limb as you admire the Creatures' light show.

iPod users can obviously plug into any of the speakers described above, but if you're the kind of person who wants everything to match, you can have fun with Altec Lansing's inMotion portable iBook speakers (www.alteclansing.com), a small battery-operated stereo system which complements and contains the iPod, folding over to make a storage/carrying case for itself! inMotion also behaves as an iPod dock for synchronisation and charging.

Accessories

So you got your laptop set up, with some edgy iTunes visuals running in full-screen mode, and your tasteful transparent speakers pumping out some AACs from your personal chillin' playlist; there's only one more thing you need – Keyspan's USB Digital Media Remote (www.keyspan.com). Plug the infrared receiver into a spare USB port, and this miniscule remote control can be configured to operate virtually any media player on your computer – Mac or PC, by assigning keyboard strokes to buttons on the remote. The receiver is also shaped to hold the remote control securely when not in use, so it won't go MIA down the back of your sofa, and if you need more buttons, the receiver can be configured to work with any JVC-compatible universal remote control.

Keyspan's Digital Media Remote.

MP3 downloads

While you're at home with your laptop, it is of course the perfect time to grab some new MP3s. Despite the best efforts of the RIAA and assorted major record labels, there are still plenty of songs by well-known artists available for free download on the internet. Debates on the rights and wrongs of file-sharing are for another book. I don't know – legally it's considered wrong at the moment ... but the record industry (ie the people feeding off the artists, not the artists themselves) have had things their way for a long time. All I really want to say about it here is be consistent – if as a musician you don't like to think of people downloading your songs without paying, then you shouldn't do it either!

- *I use Ogg Vorbis 'cause its open source and patent free, but I also can mix MP3s with TerminatorX. I use MP3s/Oggs from CDs I've already bought, 'cause I feel we still have a right to listen to our own collections on CD. I'm not a big Kazaa fan; there's plenty of good music online through the Open Music Project and the Creative Commons project, stuff that's really good and totally legal to download.*   Brian Redfern

Awkward question – what is laptop music?

- *It is the new rock and roll, although the tools are still quite 'technical'. It is electronic music outside the studio.*   SongCarver

Arguments rage about the direction, meaning, and use of digital music, and laptop music is an even-more-geeky-and-extreme offshoot of that, with its own special considerations. Some say any music that passes through a computer is digital music, that the genre war is over; others say that labelling music that way is like calling music recorded on tape '8 track music', or '24 track music' – confusing the tools with the finished work. But with computers, and I suggest especially with laptop computers, there are definitely situations where the tool is intrinsically linked with the music; there are many sounds that simply wouldn't exist without being recorded on location, and then squeezed through 98 plug-ins while the 'composer' is drinking a latte and eating chocolate cheesecake.

- *The range of music made with a laptop is so far-reaching that it's impossible really to categorise one particular area of sound under the umbrella of laptop music. The laptop, to me at least, as much as anything else is something of a convenient tool for people creating music using electronics and digital technology – certainly more convenient than numerous tape machines, minidiscs, synthesisers or samplers.*   Ergo Phizmiz

- *It tends to be put into a genre, especially with live events, because of the appearance of the 'performance'; but on a recording no-one could obviously tell whether a laptop is used or not, it might be a desktop computer or banjo that is the original source.*   Douglas Benford (musician/producer/curator)

Preparing for action

Things to deal with before you go out to play

When you take your laptop out of the house for the first time, you will experience a revelation. You will see the world in a new light – all the familiar old landmarks and points of reference will disappear. Instead your head will be full of new priorities – where can I get wifi access? Where can I sit and work without anybody hassling me? Where can I go to surreptitiously record somebody talking? And most important – where can I get a cheap cappuccino and make it last two hours? It's not all fun and games though; you have to think about protecting your investment against the elements, against accidental damage, and, on occasion, against the actions of other people.

Laptops aren't designed to be kept indoors; they need their daily exercise – but this can be a hazardous experience for a little computer. Even worse, if you're using your laptop to record or perform music, you'll be taking it into places where laptops aren't supposed to go – recording studios are okay, but pubs and clubs are a different proposition – for some reason there seem to be a lot of liquids around in those places (and lots of people full of liquid). Rowdy situations arise, accidents will happen, things get dropped. Sometimes it's true that laptops aren't as vulnerable or as delicate as you might think, but sometimes laptops are more vulnerable and delicate than you might think. Minimise the risks.

Protection

The first thing you need to do before taking your laptop out is arrange some sort of physical protection. There's nothing to stop you transporting your laptop in a plastic carrier bag, or a cheap sports holdall, and I know some people do that, and not everybody likes the idea of paying out for a dedicated case or bag, but compare the cost of a padded bag or aluminium case to the cost of repairs arising from accidental damage if your laptop takes a bashing; it's worth it – you should budget for some appropriate laptop luggage at the time you collect your new laptop.

- *I keep it snug and warm in a case. I keep it with me at all times.* Luke

- *Put it in a decent case, if it's raining outside put a few silicon crystals in the bag so no dampness penetrates.* J-Lab

A bag is usually adequate for day-to-day carry; they're lighter and more versatile than hard cases, and usually cheaper. These are either backpack or courier (over one shoulder) style, with some degree of padding, and an isolated pocket for the computer. There are plenty to choose from, ranging from anonymous no-brand models to fancier styles from brands such as Belkin (www.belkin.com), Crumpler (great looking new arrivals, www.crumpler.com), Eastpak (www.eastpak.com), Jansport (www.jansport.com), Karrimor (www.karrimor.com), Kensington (www.kensington.com), LowePro (www.lowepro.com), and Timbuk2 (www.timbuk2.com).

Sometimes a soft bag doesn't seem to offer enough protection...in a potentially more knockabout situation a metal case is a better idea, despite the extra weight and bulk. If you want to get your laptop insured then a metal, or rigid moulded, purpose-designed container is usually a condition of getting cover; they look cool, they protect your computer, and, once you've arrived at your gig, they can do useful double duty as a riser to put your computer on if you can't get it to the right height on a stand/table. Hard cases can be found all over the place, but try Samsonite (www.samsonite.com), Sumdex (www.sumdex.com), and the aptly-named Aluminium Cases (www.aluminiumcases.com).

Quote

I dropped my iBook a couple of times without any damage – they're very tough. There's a lot of rubber on those things. mindlobster

A Crumpler soft case and an aluminium case from Aluminium Cases.

Security

Something you should take very seriously if you're buying a bag is security. The plain black rectangular bags with shoulder straps and lots of zips are a dead giveaway – these are the kind of generic bags that the shared office laptop usually comes in, or that you might get free/cheap when you buy a computer. Screaming 'please steal me!', these bags should be *avoided* if you're concerned about theft!

Even though the object of our exercise is to emphasise portability and minimalism, be aware that musicians often end up carrying around more than the average laptop user, what with audio/MIDI interfaces, keyboards/controllers, headphones and cables. Make sure your bag/case is going to be roomy enough to accommodate your gear.

Check out the M-Audio Studiopack (www.m-audio.com). Designed with laptop musicians in mind, it will carry your entire 'mobile studio', accommodating large portables including Apple's 15 inch PowerBook, and has a separate compartment for a MIDI controller keyboard such as (surprise) M-Audio's own Oxygen8 or Ozone. This pack is what you might call 'pocket rich'; every inch is pocket or zip, with enough room for (quite large) interfaces, PSUs, CDs, cables, phone, and documentation. You can choose how you carry – grab handle on top, detachable shoulder strap, or backpack-style straps (which can be tucked away into a pouch). The pack is thoroughly padded, and quite rigid, so it's boxy and heavyish, but that should inspire confidence in your gear's survival. It's a poor candidate for excessive cramming, though – there's not much 'give' in those walls! I lived with the Studiopack for a few weeks, carried it everywhere I went, you definitely want to use the backpack straps – they spread the load better, and all that other ergonomic stuff.

M-Audio's essential Studiopack.

Am I talking about the Studiopack too much? It's just a bag – not intrinsically that exciting, I know, but it's what it offers that's exciting; a seductive image of you with your entire studio on your back, like an iSnail or an electro-tortoise, a portable system that you can work or jam with everywhere. There could be an army of Studiopack/laptop/Oxygen8-toting jammers out there – I'm the kind of person who can't leave home without his laptop (I hate working at home or in an office); it's always a matter of deciding what extras to carry, based on where I'm going and how long I plan to be out. The Studiopack makes these decisions easier, because you can take almost everything with you. All it needs is a dedicated storage space for headphones and it'll be perfect. M-Audio could put together a great bundle with this, some software (Reason and Live, maybe), and the Ozone or Oxygen8.

If all this fancy bag business sounds too expensive, at least consider getting some sort of zip-round semi-padded sleeve for your precious baby. There are a few of these around – try Case Logic (www.casedirect.com), Tucano (www.tucano.it) and InCase (www.goincase.com); they're relatively cheap, and you can use them to convert any bag into a laptop case. And if that's still too expensive, well ... bubble wrap.

A lot of laptop safety is down to habit. Sometimes non-believers will accuse you of being paranoid, but you should do whatever makes you feel safe, and let those other people take risks with their own computers.

Quote

Keep it with me almost always. Hide it when I can. SongCarver

- *Because my life revolves around my damned laptop I am loathe to travel with it in case of accidents, or if it gets stolen, so I only take it short distances, ie gigs in London or the occasional one-off outside London, but certainly not abroad. I have a good travel bag. If I am away from home I hide it!* Douglas Benford

And when you're out, whether it's at a cafe or at a gig, *never* repeat *never* leave your laptop unattended!

- *I have a very padded secure hard-shell briefcase to carry it around in. It always stays by my side, even when I go to the bathroom. I realise it can be gone in an instant if I turn my back to get a Coke. This is one of the drawbacks to travelling with a laptop. But I've found the advantages are well worth it.* David Das

Maybe it doesn't seem very trusting of your fellow man/woman, and I would like to live in a world where I could walk away from a PowerBook and know it would still be there when I came back, but we don't live in that world – except maybe the Swiss. Don't leave it in your car, don't go pee during a sound check and leave it unattended on stage. If you've been paying for insurance, this will be wasted if your laptop is stolen while unattended in a public place. And talking of insurance...

Insurance

- *Insurance is really difficult to get. They normally require you to keep them in a certain type of case and you can't take it out on the third Wednesday of the month; there's a lot of conditions. The best insurance is to never let it out of your sight. Get a well designed bag or a metal case. It's really important.* mindlobster

Warranty

I recommend an extended warranty on laptops. The parts are extremely expensive, and one repair will pay for the cost of the warranty. David Das

Getting 'traditional' musical instruments and gear insured for live/touring use is difficult enough, getting a laptop covered for the same uses can be almost impossible. However there are companies that have recognised the need for this protection. Music Guard (www.musicguard.co.uk) cover all kinds of musical equipment, including computers (hardware only – software won't be insured). Their site will give you an instant quote, once you've answered a few questions about how/when/where you use and transport your gear. Laptops can be covered on domestic house insurance, but you will probably have to let your insurers know you have them and check to see if they're covered; it may cost you extra.

Maintenance

I do exercise some discretion about where/when I unveil my laptop, I don't like to tempt fate. I get more nervous about using my laptop around lots of liquids, ie coffee or beer or water, than I do about somebody trying to steal it. If you're taking your laptop out a lot, you have more reason than a desktop user to backup the contents of your hard drive *regularly*.

- *I took the time to learn about technical issues. I'd much rather be riding my mountain bike than discussing protocols for your motherboard or whatever. You just learn a few things, do your maintenance, do your servicing, and that's it. I get up in the morning, open the computer up, start Norton...by the time I've had my breakfast and a shit it's done. It doesn't have to dominate your life.* J-Lab

- *Keep things clean on your desktop and filing system. Throw stuff away.* SongCarver

- *I try to keep the machine clear from freeware things and mysterious downloads.* Eavesdropper

- *A well tuned machine makes me more productive for sure.* JDG

- *For me it's about avoiding problems. I think maintenance is really important.* mindlobster

This is where you can mentally insert all of the usual computer related talk about disk utilities, crash prevention, crash recovery, etc. It's not laptop specific, and I want to get on to other matters. Just remember to disable any scheduled indexing/backup routines before a gig or critical recording session – you don't want them slowing down your laptop while you're in full flow.

'The iBook went back when the drive bearings got noisy, which is apparently a common problem with the curvy iBooks. That was pretty good – it was still under guarantee so Apple sent it to Germany or wherever, it came back very quickly and they also fixed a couple of other things that I hadn't mentioned...like the CD tray was cracked and they fixed that which was nice. Apple are good with that stuff, again maybe it's in the repairs that you see more of the advantages of having a computer and OS put together by the same company." – mindlobster

- *I've been very disciplined and stopped putting my coffee on top of the (closed) laptop.* IriXx

Storage

If you're going to be a good boy/girl and back up your data, you need something to back up on to. For long term storage it's safest to use CDRs or DVDRs. For short to medium term you can use external hard drives. Because this book's about portability, I'm going to concentrate on bus-powered drives – you can take it with you . The bus-power thing is also useful because a fast external drive can be used to record onto, so you ought to have a drive that lets you do it all on the move!

French company Lacie (www.lacie.com) produce the cutest portable drives around, and they work pretty well too! Lacie are never slow when it comes to adopting new developments, and they have produced drives using USB1, FireWire, and now USB2 and FireWire 800, including bus-powered models.

The latest version of their famous Pocket Drive, with its distinctive silicon shock-proof bumper, is the Pocket Drive U&I, featuring FireWire 400 and USB 1/2 connections. The Pocket Drive measures 143x87x25mm, and is available in capacities of 40, 60 and 80GB, with a variety of rotational speeds. Lacie update their hard-

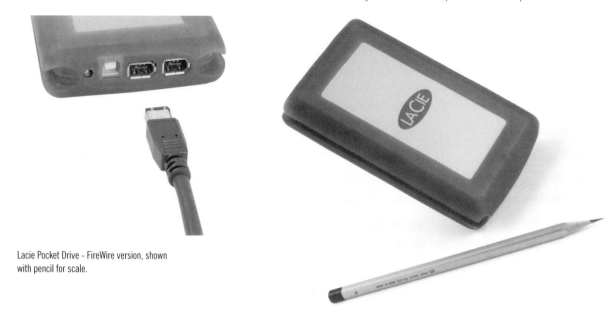

Lacie Pocket Drive - FireWire version, shown with pencil for scale.

Lacie DataBank - designed by F.A. Porsche.

ware all the time though, so by the time you read this – who knows? 'Designed for today's business traveller", it says in the blurb, but don't worry – you can use them too! Lacie's latest, most minimal, and most bling-oriented drive (it is shaped like an ingot) is the Databank; this magnesium-cased cutie was designed by F.A.Porsche, and is very small: 111x63x13mm, but still manages storage capacities of 5/10/20GB using, again, FireWire and USB1/2.

Like it says in those ads for the 'Radio Times' – 'other portable storage devices are available'; for example SmartDisk (www.smartdisk.com) and Archos (www.archos.com) have ranges of FireWire USB2 drives with capacities ranging from 20-80GB, and the universally handy iPod could be perceived as an external HD that doubles as an MP3/AAC player.

The SmartDisk FireLite FireWire drive.

Treat your iPod as an external HD.

iPod bit

The current model iPods have capacities up to 40GB, and FireWire/USB2 connections. You could treat your iPod as an external HD that also happens to be a MP3/AAC/AIF/WAV player – use, say, 10GB for your songs and 30GB for your data.

Recording media such as CDR and DVDR are fairly safe for storage, but not 100% reliable; they can fail. It's also possible that they could be taken by fire or theft, or miscellaneous accident. Make two copies of your archive disks, and keep them in different locations – not different places in your bedroom, not different rooms in your house, but in different buildings. Ask a friend – a few disks don't take up much room, nobody should object. If you've got a friend who needs to do the same thing, swap with them.

You can make an external USB HD really cheaply if you've got an old HD around – maybe one you pulled out when upgrading your laptop. There are caddies available for 'spare' drives which will turn them into fully functioning USB bus-powered external drives. These are mostly no-brand items, and can be found anywhere that sells PC accessories, although Belkin (www.belkin.com) produce a more sophisticated USB2 version.

Backup is important. Having a big HD inside your laptop is no excuse, you must backup outside your laptop!

Belkin USB2 hard drive case.

Power tripping

One of your new preoccupations will be battery life. 'How long will they last? Is there anywhere I can plug in to the mains?' Well, don't get your hopes up on that last one; you'll be *amazed* at how hostile people get when you try to 'steal' their electricity. If they get a sniff of a plug going into one of their mains sockets, you will transform from a welcomed guest/valued customer/respected patron, to a terrorist/master criminal/wife beater all in one. This comes from personal experience at several different locations, including joints that brag regularly in their advertising about offering wifi access for laptop users. They freak out – I have witnessed a member of staff literally screaming at a hapless laptop user who thought they might just plug in for a few minutes.

But sometimes it can be done. Plug into the wall and see if anybody notices – just as the episodes I mentioned above happened, so I have met people who are very kind and accommodating, especially if you are a regular customer, and buy a coffee periodically, and are nice and polite. Support your local coffee shop and they might support you!

A more reliable bet is to carry some extra power yourself, in the shape of a second battery. It's expensive, and it means carrying more weight, but if you like to travel a lot, a second battery is a better investment than fancy accessories like MIDI controllers or interfaces. Just remember to charge it before going out – that's the most frustrating thing…you get somewhere, battery uno goes flat, hey, no prob, unpack battery dos – oops!

Laptop batteries seldom deliver the claimed charge time anyway. Some users get resentful about this, and feel they've been cheated, but real-world battery life figures are impossible to give. Maybe there's a bit of marketing hype at play, but there are so many variables – how can a manufacturer test for every combination of environment and usage?

There are some simple things you can do to preserve battery life. Shut down all unused applications – there are cases where launching one music application will start up various background activities. For example, if you have Unity Session installed on your Mac, it will start running in the background when you open any other MIDI application, taking a share of your CPU and RAM, using your computer's resources when you don' t want it to. Reduce the number of colours in your display from 'millions' to 'thousands'. Reduce the brightness of your display. Disconnect/deactivate unused peripherals, including internal add-ons, such as wireless cards.

Plan your trip around battery life. When your computer tells you 'one hour remaining' don't expect to get that much working time, it'll shut down or go to sleep before then. Don't get caught short!

Info

David Das is a performer/producer who plays hundreds of gigs each year, with a laptop at the core of his minimal stage setup.

The David Das live rig – in his own words

Since 1999 I've been on the road playing keyboards and driving a computer-based live show from an onstage computer. I'm often asked about my live rig, which is a lightweight, portable, yet powerful keyboard rig with virtually unlimited possibilities. I literally travel with a Mac laptop, a relatively small controller keyboard (a Roland XP-30), an audio interface, a MIDI interface, and cables. I've found that it's not necessary for me to lug around a huge rig with keyboards and modules up the wazoo. I've only got two hands, after all. Sounds that I like from vintage or other keyboards, I sample and trigger onstage. Some sounds I custom-program using software synthesisers. Others, I'll play directly from the Roland, which has a good palette of bread-and-butter sounds.

MOTU's Digital Performer is my main digital audio sequencer, driving the entire stage show. I also use the Native Instruments B4 and Absynth software synthesisers. The B4 is a killer emulation of a Hammond B3 (sounds better than any other emulation I've ever heard) and Absynth is a synthesiser capable of sounds like nothing else in the world.

As far as wiring and connections, my rig is fairly simple. MIDI is sent out from my controller keyboard into either a MOTU Fastlane USB or a MOTU MIDI Timepiece AV MIDI interface, then the MIDI interface is connected via USB to the Macintosh. This is so that I can play the B4 or Absynth or other software synths.

When it comes to audio, I send six channels out from my rig. Outputs 1-2 are a stereo pair straight out of the Roland keyboard. This is my backup plan in case anything should go wrong; I'll always be able to play the keyboard. Outputs 3-4 are another stereo pair containing loops, pre-recorded keyboard parts, and software synths, all coming out of the computer via a multichannel FireWire interface (I use a Metric Halo Mobile I/O for this purpose). Outputs 5-6 are two mono outputs also coming out of the FireWire interface. Output 5 is a 'count' channel that contains a vocal countoff to each song that is sent to all the band members and singers in their in-ear monitors. It also contains audio pitches for one song that starts a cappella . That way, no drummer countoff is necessary, and the entire band can start simultaneously with no outside cues (which looks very cool from an audience perspective!). Output 6 is an actual click channel, sent to the drummer and also to myself, partially because I like to play to the click, but also because it's my first warning just in case anything goes wrong with the computer.

I've been fortunate enough to have never experienced any serious computer-related problems onstage, and this is the number one question I'm asked: how do you make sure the computer is stable and won't crash on you? My first answer is that I partition my drive and designate a special 1 gigabyte partition as my Live Rig. This partition contains its own OS (only installed with its minimum components) plus the software I need for onstage use (Digital Performer, the B4, Absynth, and hardware drivers). This insures that I don't have any stray extra extensions from internet apps or other things that I have installed on my normal working partition. MOTU writes very stable software, and I've never had a software crash on stage.

Lately we've been working with video sync quite a bit. Other notables in the industry such as Madonna, Nine Inch Nails, and Cher also use Digital Performer onstage and integrate video into their stage shows. After looking at their set-ups, we found a way to integrate perfectly synced video, driven from a second Mac offstage, and projected up above the stage during performance. A SMPTE track for each song was pre-recorded out of my stage computer and added as the audio track of the video playing on the offstage Mac. So for performance, we connect the audio out of the offstage Mac into the SMPTE in of the stage Mac, and I turn on external sync for the songs that need video.

David's gloriously minimal onstage rig.

Thus, the offstage Mac is actually in the driver's seat for the songs that have video. All the audio still comes from my machine, which saves us the extra trouble of setting up more channels to send to FOH (front of house). We actually designed a unique drum solo for the drummer, Jeff Bowders. Jeff wrote a special double-kit drum solo, then shot video of himself playing one of the two parts. This video was projected on to the video screen and played back along with its corresponding audio and original click track, as he played the second kit part live on stage. The video was projected on a screen above his head. So he got the chance to play a double drum solo with himself. (Since writing this, David is preparing to move to Mac OSX, possibly incorporating Ableton Live into his rig.)

Doing it – with hardware and software

What is this chapter about?

You're ready to take your laptop out beyond your front door – it's about time!

Other than for studio-specific tasks, such as mixing, where you definitely need to be tied to some heavy duty equipment (ie proper speakers – don't try and mix on headphones!), pretty much the entire laptop jamming/writing/recording experience can be indulged on the move – with the help of a few carefully chosen extras. The funny thing is, being at home should be ideal, but it's so easy to get distracted, there are always things to do, whether work things or play things. Being outdoors, even if it's in a busy coffee shop or someplace, with a lot of people coming and going, maybe even with music playing in the background – somehow that can actually help; the change of scene, the people-watching – it can all be beneficial. And if you really can't get those creative juices flowing, maybe some caffeine-type stimulation will help...

- *Just get out, go somewhere different. If you want to write some low slung booty bass go to some place where you can look at plenty of women walking past on a summer's day.* J-Lab

In the following pages I'll look at hardware, software and accessories that you might find useful for laptop music. The applied standards are flexible – there's not always a 'yes or no' answer as to whether something's laptop-friendly or not, and obviously there's a lot of general computer music products that you can use anyway. You might be surprised at some of the inclusions/omissions – well remember, a lot of it's about personal opinion and experience; some of these decisions were quite arbitrary, based on such carefully considered factors as personal experience, asking other laptop musicians what they thought, and what mood I was in at the time. It's quite freeflowing, like the activity of laptop music itself. But hey, it gives us a starting point, a structure to work with, and that should be enough. When you write *your* book you can do this stuff however you like.

- *If you tend to use software that doesn't have a characteristic sound, or you get to know it well enough that you can steer it away from the obvious presets, then that's a good thing. That's always been a problem with synths anyway, you try out a synth in the shop and you get a great preset with tons of effects on it, and first you tend to use that instead of editing it and creating your own sounds. With Ableton Live – it doesn't make any sounds, it can only use what you load into it, though some people still manage to make it sound like it's*

43

coming off a demo CD! I think they tried really hard on that application to get away from that kind of thing; they actually ask people to let them know if they're doing things other than techno. mindlobster

Doing it ... with hardware

- *Because I worked with a limited amount of equipment for a long time, I got into finding out what it couldn't do and reconciling that with what it could do. There is that advantage of working with limitations – you can do amazing things...* J-Lab

- *Don't underestimate the convenience of bus-powered devices, battery powered mics, etc. There are many times when you can capture an amazing performance/sound by whipping out your gear quickly.* SongCarver

Some people seem to think FireWire means laptop-friendly. it doesn't. Laptop-friendly hardware is bus-powered. That's it.

- *Back in the mid '90s I used to use a laptop with the dos version of Cakewalk and an old serial MIDI interface to sequence MIDI, but the amount of gear you had to lug around made it less than a convenient musical experience. With the advent of more powerful processors and the 'desktop replacement' machine, now you have good enough performance to use software synthesis, so it's possible to perform everything, with software, on a laptop.* Brian Redfern

If you can't take it with you everywhere you go, and use whenever you feel like it, what's the point? That's how I've approached the hardware in this section – everything here is bus-powered. Puritanical as this sounds, I admit I have cheated a little – there are more 'studio bound' pieces that are still likely to interest laptop users, so I've jammed them into a short section called 'Studio Special' in Chapter 5.

Let's think about what you might pack for a day out – laptop, yep sure, that's easy for you to say (I forgot my laptop once and arrived at a session with a bag full of accessories but no PowerBook – oops!); spare battery if you got one; you may not need much else, it depends on what kind of work you're doing. The most immediate requirement is for a compact and comfortable set of headphones, and maybe some kind of MIDI keyboard or controller.

With keyboards and controllers, the whole concept of 'portable' comes into question. How 'portable' is a keyboard which measures 420x230x80mm and weighs 1.8kg? That depends on the size of your pack/bag, and how much you're willing to carry.

You should aim to carry the minimum of stuff. It's like being one of those mountain climbers, or a pro cyclist. Minimalism is its own reward, and everything has to justify its place in the backpack – there ought to be some kind of weight to usefulness formula that we could apply when shopping for new gear. I've tried to apply this techno-minimalist philosophy consistently, looking for things that somehow fulfil the criteria, things that fit the laptop music ideal...

Audio interfaces

Small, lightweight, bus-powered audio interfaces are a boon to laptop users. If your laptop has a clean sound output, then you may not need any other soundcards or interfaces for an average day out. However, if you're using good quality headphones, or if you monitor on good quality speakers, you will notice the difference when you step up to an audio interface.

Laptop audio interfaces come in assorted flavours – USB1/2, FireWire400 and PC Cardbus. They each have their pros and cons: USB1 – cheap/low bandwidth; USB2 – high bandwidth/rarity value (though this will doubtless change soon); FireWire400 – high bandwidth/more expensive; PC Card – high bandwidth/needs the PC Card slot!

USB audio interfaces are great because they're cheap, simple to configure, and USB is almost universal. They can be prone to mysterious compatibility problems, though – you need to try before you buy if possible – and they are best used in non-critical situations. If you can live with the shortcomings, however (depends on how you like to work and how much cash you've got), then they are very useful little things; here's a few, in cavalier skimming style:

The Griffin Technology iMic (www.griffintechnology.com), which I mentioned in Chapter 2 'Listening', is one of the cheapest and lightest USB options, giving Mac users (sorry, it's Mac only) a clean headphone-out and a stereo-in with the minimum of messing. It doesn't require any drivers, and has no onboard controls at all – any adjustments you make have to be either outside the computer or in your software.

- *Sometimes I'll interact at home with the bass – I'll be playing along with the bass going straight through the laptop.* J-Lab

Edirol (www.edirol.com) have an ever-changing line-up of USB audio gear – at the moment they have four bus-powered interfaces in their range. The most basic model is the UA-1A, a simple stereo in/out, and an SP/DIF version, the UA-1D, is also available. The UA-3D gets more complex, with mic, stereo, SP/DIF and instrument inputs, and outputs for stereo, headphones, and SP/DIF. Hands-on control is available via separate controls for guitar/mic and stereo inputs. The UA-20 is the same but different, as they say, with guitar/mic/stereo in, and outputs for headphones, stereo, and SP/DIF. The major differences are the lack of separate volume controls for guitar/mic and stereo, and the addition of MIDI in/out.

Edirol UA-1D USB/digital audio interface.

Edirol UA-3D USB audio interface

Edirol UA-20 USB audio/MIDI interface

(For those with older MIDI equipment that they want to use with their computer, Edirol – and others – also produce MIDI/USB interfaces, often quite simple devices like the UM-1 with 1x MIDI in/out at one end, and USB at the other. Although this might contradict the 'bus-powered' ethic, there are times when other MIDI gear can be useful – like maybe a battery powered keyboard, or external hardware sequencers.)

Edirol UM-1 USB/MIDI interface.

Tascam's US-122 (www.tascam.co.uk) is probably the smallest USB interface to feature stereo, instrument, MIDI in/out AND phantom powered XLRs for mic input. Tascam also have the US-224, with a mixer-style interface and plenty input options – MIDI, SP/DIF, stereo, line instrument, and two phantom powered XLRs. Yes this is bus-powered, not to be confused with Tascam's mains-only 428!

The Digidesign MBox (www.digidesign.com) is an interesting one. There's a lot of snob value in the Digidesign name and its Pro Tools associations, and indeed the MBox comes bundled with Pro Tools LE. Originally Mac OS9 only, the MBox now supports Mac OSX and Windows XP. Although the MBox requires ProTools LE to work, PT's Rewire support makes it possible to use other audio apps simultaneously, and the MBox is bundled with no-frills versions of Reason, Live, Sampletank, Amplitude, and T-Racks.

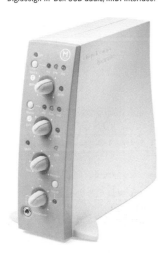
Digidesign M-Box USB audio/MIDI interface.

The MBox has stereo line and SP/DIF input and two XLR phantom powered mic inputs with Focusrite preamps. This will appeal to on-a-budget recordists, but also perhaps to ProTools users who have a full studio system at HQ, and want something familiar and compatible when they're working in the field. If you need more storage, Glyph (www.glyphtech.com) do a matching FireWire hard drive. Nice!

Mackie's Spike (www.mackie.com) is designed along similar principles to the MBox – a cute-looking, do-it-all bus powered USB interface; the main difference is that it's not tied to any particular sequencer. It also comes with an excellent software bundle – a no-frills (again) version of Ableton Live, and a full version of Raw

Material's outstanding Tracktion sequencer. Spike has two mic/line/instrument inputs, and onboard EQ and dynamics control – very useful for controlling your signal before it gets in the computer, at the same time saving your CPU from doing some extra work – always a good idea!

There are USB audio interfaces whose sole purpose is to give the maximum possible number of outputs – I'm talking about the eMagic A26 (www.emagic.com), with 2 in/6 out and SP/DIF, and the ESI Pro GIGAport AG (www.esi-pro.com) with 2 in/8 out. These devices are basic in function and minimalist in appearance; they're trying to squeeze a lot out of USB – I'd feel safer on stage with a FireWire device handling that many outputs.

If you ARE going to stick with USB: the USB audio interface for those in the know is the Apogee Mini-Me (www.apogeedigital.com). Costing several times more than its nearest rival, the Apogee emphasises quality over quantity – it's a simple 2x mic/line pre-amp designed to do its job as cleanly as possible. Like Spike, Mini-Me starts working on your signal before your audio even enters the computer, with a built-in stereo compressor/limiter. Word of mouth is good, and some broadcasters have elected to use the Mini-Me for location recording. I would love to tell you that I've used this thing, and that it's definitely worth the price (or definitely NOT worth the price, come to think of it), but sadly review examples are in short supply, so your guess is as good as mine on this one.

Apogee Mini-Me - high-end USB audio.

The MBox and Spike and Mini-Me probably represent state-of-the-art USB1 audio; there's got to be a limit to how far it's worth going with the format. Manufacturers would be better devoting their attention to USB2 and FireWire devices. Talking of FireWire...

The MOTU 828 (www.motu.com) was the first FireWire audio device to have any 'mass market' appeal, and FireWire/laptop owners bought them and used

MOTU 828 MKII FireWire audio/MIDI interface.

Presonus FIREstation - FireWire
audio/MIDI/MLan.

Presonus FIREstation - FireWire
audio/MIDI/MLan.

them, despite being resentful of the unit's bulk and need for mains power. The
Presonus (www.presonus.com) FIREstation upped the ante with MIDI and MLan
compatibility (more on the MOTU 828 and FIREstation in 'Studio Special') – but is
unfortunately still bus-powered and in bulky rack-mount format.

- *I use two Metric Halo interfaces which, to me, are the ultimate in portability.
  One is eight-in/eight-out with lots of digital I/O, the other is two-in/two-out.*
  David Das

Metric Halo's Mobile I/O (www.mhlabs.com) was the first to break the bus-power
barrier, albeit in an expensive way. If you want no-questions-asked quality in a true
laptop-friendly package, then this is still the one to go for, especially if (a) you've
got a pro-sized budget, and (b) you want something of gig-quality construction.

The Mobile I/O can be rack-mounted, but will also sit neatly under a 15'
PowerBook. Due to its size, it's not so friendly for carrying around in a bag all day,
but if you've got some transportation other than the bus, this still counts as
portable! The Mobile I/O features eight inputs, eight outputs, comprehensive mixing software, and onboard FX. Like the Apogee Mini-Me, review examples of the
Mobile I/O were thin on the ground at the time of writing, so I don't really know
any more than you do. But drool, drool.

Despite the I/O's portability, a gap remained – there was a need for a compact,
portable device that wouldn't accept the compromises of USB bandwidth. Enter the
M-Audio FireWire 410 (www.m-audio.com).

M-Audio FW410 – FireWire audio/MIDI
interface, and it's bus-powered!

This is a sweet one; probably the device I was most enthusiastic about featuring in this book. It's incredibly useful, which is why you'll see it's name mentioned
so often within these pages; if it came down to it and I could only point you towards
two essential laptop music products, they would be the FW410 and Ableton Live
(conveniently a basic version of Live is included in the FW410 package).

The FW410's front panel gives you two mic/instrument/line preamps with phantom power and independent gain controls, two headphone sockets with independent volume controls, an output level controller, power on/off, phantom power on/off,
and MIDI thru (enabling the FW410 to pass MIDI signals when powered 'off').

Round back are a power supply socket (for when the FW410 is connected to a
laptop with a four-pin FireWire output – they won't power the unit in the way that
the six-pin type does), MIDI in and out, two FireWire ports (so further FireWire
devices can be daisy chained), SP/DIF in/out (in coaxial and toslink forms), eight
analogue line outputs, and two analogue inputs (the FW410 supports resolutions
of up to 24bit/96KHz). That's a lot of connections for a small box. A control panel

and software mixer are installed, which makes quite complex routing possible, and chosen configurations can be saved for subsequent recall.

I used the FW410 with monitors, headphones, and microphones, and in a setup with an Oxygen8 connected to my laptop's USB port, and a FireWire webcam connected to the FW410's second FireWire port. Although M-Audio don't recommend chaining non-bus powered devices, I didn't experience any problems when the camera was attached; Ableton Live, which I was using at the time, continued to work fine with the Oxygen8 and the FW410, and Arkaos was still able to recognise the FireWire webcam (even when the FW410 was 'off'; as long as it remained connected, the webcam still worked). This is the perfect setup if you want to run the Arkaos/Live combo with webcam feed all on one machine! I'll be trying it at my next gig.

Under Mac OSX I had no problems getting any applications to recognise the FW410; DeKstasy, Live, Metro, Reason, Session, Tracktion and Traktor all behaved as expected, with pre-listen available where advertised. The only problem I experienced with the FW410 was that the computer sometimes had problems identifying it when first connected – this was with Mac OS 10.2.6 and the latest available version of the FW410 drivers. However, once the FW410 did get talking to the laptop, it was consistent and trouble-free.

Headphone jamming with the FW410 and two laptops

Thanks to its separate headphone outputs and bus power, the FW410 can be used to facilitate on-location jamming between two laptops, with independent volume controls for each participant.

One of the laptops – let's call it Laptop A – must have FireWire, and have the FW410 drivers installed. The other – Laptop B – only needs a headphone out (and of course some music software – I'm assuming we're using Ableton Live for this jam).

1   Connect the FW410 to Laptop A.
2   Get a mini jack stereo-to-left/right 1/4' jacks 'y' lead. Connect the mini jack stereo out to Laptop B's headphone socket, and the left/right jacks to the FW410's analog inputs 1/2.
3   Connect a pair of headphones to each of the FW410's headphone outputs.
4   Launch Ableton Live on Laptop A.
5   Launch Ableton Live on Laptop B.
6   On Laptop A select FW410 as output and input device.
7   On Laptop A select Live as input type in the 'in type' box in the in/out window.
8   Immediately below that select 'FireWire 410 multichannel 1/2' as input channel, and click the monitoring button for that track.
9   Start a Live clip playing on Laptop B and you should see an input level on Laptop A.
10 Get jammin, and remember you have individual control over your headphone levels. Obviously this kind of setup will work with other interfaces, and other applications. In the past I've bodged together similar setups with two iBooks, an iMic, and a stereo headphone splitter, but something like the FW410 is necessary to give true independent volume control.

The FW410 is flexible, all right. It can be used to create a separate headphone mix for an artist while recording, and AC3 and DTS surround support is available via the digital outputs. Zero latency monitoring is possible (though as usual when people use this term they're really talking about monitoring the input signal only, NOT the entire mix), though I found latency when monitoring the mix low anyway, and when recording vocals through some plug-ins I was able to monitor the processed signal without having to listen to the clean input too. Low latency software monitoring is also possible with ASIO drivers, but as a Mac OSX user I wasn't able to test this!

I hope M-Audio will resolve the driver problem soon – the only other complaints I have are minor: the protruding knobs on the front panel need protection in transit, and it could come with a longer FireWire cable. I suggest M-Audio make some sort of small padded zip-up case available, and follow it up with a matching FireWire hard drive that stacks with the FW410, like the one that Glyph make for Digidesign's MBox.

The FW410 is a perfect example of a versatile, high quality, and *laptop relevant* product. It has a clearly defined function, it's small enough to carry around, it uses high bandwidth FireWire instead of golfball-through-a-hosepipe USB1 (is that the expression?), and, crucially, it's bus-powered, so you can truly take it anywhere!

Is it worth the money? Does it justify its place in our oh-so-limited-space laptop bag? Yes and yes. It's a beautiful thing, it looks great, and it works great. It's small and understated, but you feel you're getting your money's worth. Peace and love, FW410!

(Still, I think there is a place for a little stereo in/out FireWire bus-powered interface with the simplest functionality – just clean, easy, and a lot of headroom for stereo. Guess I'll have to wait and see...)

If your laptop has the old PC Card/Cardbus slot (and many still do), then you've the option of using that for your audio connections. The cheapest way into this is Echo's Indigo (www.echoaudio.com) range, which possess all of our required virtues – simplicity, effectiveness, and affordability. There are three cards in the series – collect em all! Er, I mean choose from the Indigo (basic stereo out with volume control), the Indigo IO (stereo in and out), and Indigo DJ (two distinct stereo outputs with separate volume levels, designed for prelistening). Which one you choose is a decision only you can make. The DJ seems kinda sexy, but I don't do enough of that DJ-type gigging; the IO doesn't give enough controls for recording – if I wanted to just improve the quality of my output, then the basic Indigo is the one I'd go for.

If you need slightly more sophisticated connections on a PC Card, then you should look at Digigram's VX Pocket cards (www.digigram.com). The VXPocket V2 has breakout XLR cables for two mono inputs and two mono outputs, while the VXPocket 440 has four inputs and four outputs. Each card also has a stereo SP/DIF input and output. Linux users will be gratified to know that Linux drivers come as standard with these cards.

Echo Indigo PC Card interface - basic stereo out.

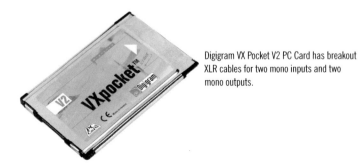

Digigram VX Pocket V2 PC Card has breakout XLR cables for two mono inputs and two mono outputs.

Keyboards

The strange challenge faced by desktop musicians everywhere. Just as you begin to enjoy the convenience of having your entire studio neatly contained within the drive of your Mac/PC, and making statements like 'yeah it's great, all you need to take to gigs is your laptop', then you start craving external hardware which will let you control the software. It's true – some things just aren't the same without a little knob twiddling along the way.

Using an interface like a keyboard or other controller will have a positive effect on your sound and performance, and if you're only going to have one MIDI controller, you're better off with a keyboard than anything else. Until something radically better comes along, there's nothing as useful to the computer musician as a MIDI keyboard. Even if, like me, you can only play one-fingered clod style, it makes a great control interface. Keyboards are versatile – they can be used to enter notes, drum parts, trigger events on/off – those keys don't have to represent notes, they can send all kinds of MIDI information.

After a slow start, there are many bus-powered USB/MIDI keyboards around. Some of them are purely keyboards, some have more controller functions, with added knobs and faders, and some double as audio interfaces.

As far as I know, M-Audio's Oxygen8 was the first bus-powered USB/MIDI keyboard. It's a chubby looking silver unit, with twenty-five keys, pitch and modulation wheels, eight controller knobs, one fader, and a smattering of buttons. The 'piano' keys double as multifunction data entry keys. The Oxygen8 can also be powered by batteries or mains power, for times when you want to use it with other MIDI hardware, but we won't dwell on that here.

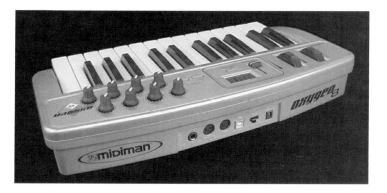

M-Audio Oxygen8 - USB-powered MIDI keyboard.

Mapping MIDI notes and controllers to music software can be easy; it depends on how friendly your software is. Each knob can be assigned to send different MIDI controller data on different channels, and there are five user presets, so you can save setups for different applications. I've never needed to use the presets, because I tend to only work with 1 or 2 apps at once, and it suits me to use the same settings for all of them.

Because style matters

If you don't like silver on your keyboards, visit *www.nativeinstruments.com* and order the Oxygen8 NI edition – it's blue!

For me, one of the most useful things about the Oxygen8 is the MIDI out port on the back. I found that I could connect an Edirol UM-1 MIDI/USB interface to this, and use it to send MIDI to a second computer simultaneously – very useful for controlling two apps at once; in my case it was Ableton Live on one laptop, and Arkaos on the other (see Chapter 6 – Adding Video for more on this setup).

The Oxygen8 is an important addition to the mobile studio. At first I didn't carry it around too much, because I didn't have a bag it would fit in – this is where we again encounter the 'definition of portability' issue. Once I started carrying it around in M-Audio's tailor-made Studiopack, however, I began to appreciate the Oxygen8's finer qualities.

If in doubt ... cheat

I don't need my Oxygen8 to look pretty, I need it to work! So, because I use mine to trigger scenes in Live and movies in Arkaos simultaneously, I made things easy for myself and labelled all the keys with masking tape and marker pen, numbered 1-25. The scenes in my Live set are numbered the same way - I find 25 scenes is enough for one song. When I get to the end of the song I send channel and program changes from the Oxygen8 and then it's straight into the next song (I prefer to keep all of my Live songs in the same file, otherwise I wouldn't need to bother with changing channels in this way).

If you like the Oxygen8 but need more than 25 keys for some reason (like you can actually play chords and stuff) then check out the Oxygen8's big brother, Radium, available in 49 and 61 key versions. The Radium is essentially an Oxygen8 with more keys and the addition of eight faders – less portable, but still bus-powered for those summertime park jams (and see 'Studio Special' for information on the Oxygen8's and Radium's close relative, the Ozone).

Oxygen8's big brother – Radium, if you need more than 25 keys.

It was just a matter of time before the Oxygen8 was followed by similar products. Evolution's MK series (www.evolution.co.uk) follows the same path as the Oxygen8, down to that useful MIDI output (although with ten, rather than five, memory presets). The major differences between the Evolution MK225C and the Oxygen8 are cosmetic, though the Evolution does have the advantage of requiring fewer button presses to send program and channel changes – useful onstage.

Evolution also go bigger than just 25 keys. The MK249C has, yes, 49 keys (and 12 knobs), and then there's the matter of the MK361 – 61 keys and 16 knobs; although bus-powered and quite light, it's questionable as to whether this big keyboard counts as 'portable'. The MK249C and MK361C are also available without controller knobs and minus the 'C' suffix, but I'm telling you, the knobs are essential.

In use, the Evolutions don't feel as substantial as the M-Audio Oxygen8, but they're still perfectly workable. I guess if you're the more, er, flamboyant or just plain violent and aggressive performer, then these keyboards can be viewed as disposable. Instruments like these don't offer a high-end piano or synth playing experience, but to complain about that would be missing the point somewhat.

And now there are even more entries in the USB/MIDI keyboard arms race. Edirol's PCR-30 and PCR-50 (www.edirol.com) each have eight knobs and eight faders, as well as a modulation stick, and a V-Link connection, which is used to communicate with Edirol's highly expensive and ultra-cool DV-7PR video presentation hardware.

Edirol PCR-30 – USB-powered MIDI keyboard.

I would surely like to spend some quality time with Novation's ReMOTE 25 Audio (www.novationmusic.com, ReMOTE 25 also available without audio features) – another 25-key unit, but larger than other 25-key models, because it has to accommodate so many features: audio interface with two mic preamps and phantom power, onboard effect processor, SP/DIF output, X-Y touchpad (this is a great idea!), pitch/mod/joystick, LCD display, 64 presets, 28 buttons, 8 sliders, 16 pots, and 3 encoders. In terms of construction and features this is a different proposition from the other keyboards mentioned here, and the price reflects it.

At 468 x 68 x 278mm, and with a semi-weighted keyboard, the ReMOTE 25 feels like a 'real' synth; it's somewhat larger than, say, the Oxygen8, which I feel to be at the size limit for a genuinely portable keyboard. But I guess it depends what you're used to, and how you like to travel, and as I haven't tried one yet I better keep my trap shut.

Novation ReMOTE 25 Audio – USB-powered MIDI keyboard/audio interface.

Controllers

There are all kinds of dedicated controllers out there; MIDI keyboards for instance – we just talked about them, where were you? And there have always been other choices; various hardware sequencers that send MIDI from their interfaces, and mains-powered knob boxes, such as the Keyfax Phat Boy (www.keyfax.com) and Kenton's Control Freak (www.kentonuk.com).

But now laptop jammers have better, more specific options...and truly portable ones at that.

Evolution's UC33 (www.evolution.co.uk) is one of the best-equipped USB/MIDI control units around. It's bus-powered, of course, and is crammed with control options. If you don't need a keyboard, then this has to be your first choice. It has 9 faders (each with a green LED), 24 knobs, and 28 buttons (including sequencer-type transport controls), topped off with a relatively large blue LCD screen; all those lights make the UC33 much easier to use on a gloomy stage. All of the UC33's controllers can be assigned to different channels, and to send whatever MIDI info you require. It has 33 presets, so in total you're looking at – a lot of assignable, saveable, controls.

Evolution UC-33 – USB-powered MIDI controller.

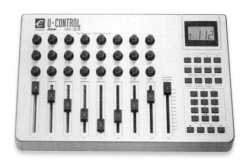

The UC33 will work with anything that receives MIDI – synths, samplers, sequencers, lighting rigs; it's highly flexible. The UC33 is supplied with a set of plastic template overlay sheets for commonly-used music apps (a blank is included if you want to make your own). I tried it with Live first, but found the Oxygen8 preferable for use with that particular app. I tried it with Arkaos, and it was pretty good. Then I tried it with Native Instruments' Traktor DJ (www.nativeinstruments.com), and it rocked – it's like they were made for each other. The number and type of controllers on the UC33's surface correspond beautifully well to Traktor's interface, and I recommend the combination to any laptop DJ (there's more on Traktor/UC33 in Chapter 7 – The Laptop DJ).

The UC33 solves a lot of problems...it's not small or light, but it's still compact enough for daily carry.

For those who think the UC33 is too complex, or too big, or too expensive, there is the UC16. It's more like other knobby controller boxes on the market – a simple box with two parallel rows of eight knobs, an LCD display, and a numeric keypad. The rear panel features a MIDI out port, on/off switch, mains power input for standalone use, and of course a USB port. The UC16 is heavier than it looks, but that's what we call reassuring. Like the UC33, it has memory presets (25), and each knob can be independently configured.

While the UC16 is a significant improvement over trying to jam or improvise music with a trackpad and a qwerty keyboard, it lacks the far-reaching possibilities of the UC33. If you just want to control virtual knobs, the UC16 is fine, and it will increase your performance options, but the UC33 is the boss.

If you don't like MIDI keyboards or controllers, but you want something to help you add a performance element to your laptop horseplay, then I've got good news and bad news for you. The goods news is that there are many other options; the bad news is that most of these are fiddly to set up, are self-build jobs, or are expensive specialist items.

Here's a semi-random list of other MIDI control options. You might find something that starts you off on an interesting path; to each his own...

Battery-powered drum pads. I've got a set with MIDI-out that used to belong to Brian Eno – name-dropping is fun! If you like to hit things rather than type you should try it. www.yamaha.com

Guitar/bass/wind-to MIDI converters. If you're an instrumentalist who wants to combine his skills with what software has to offer. www.yamaha.com

Chapman Stick. This distinctive looking (and sounding) instrument is available to order with a Roland MIDI pickup, which works on guitars too, but this is an interesting combination. www.chapmanstick.com, www.roland.com.

Yamaha WX5 MIDI wind controller - you never know...

Chapman Stick fitted with Roland MIDI pickup (left).

Chapman Stick/Roland MIDI pickup detail (right).

Ribbon control. Great for effects manipulation, but you can go further and use it to play notes, or send any MIDI info for unusual results. See the Kurzweil Expression Mate, for example www.kurzweilmusicsystems.com.

Body Synth. Use your body movement to control MIDI – www.synthzone.com/bsynth.html.

The Continuum Fingerboard. It's like a giant ribbon controller – www.cerlsoundgroup.org/Continuum/

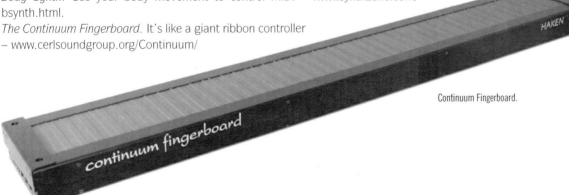

Continuum Fingerboard.

Soundbeam.

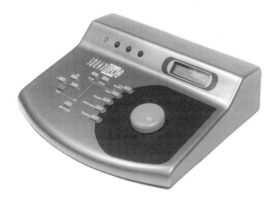

Sound Beam. Beam-based movement-to-MIDI interface. www.soundbeam.co.uk

Going back to the smaller, cheaper way of doing things; if you're using an application like Ableton Live that allows you to assign qwerty keyboard characters to specific functions, you can use non-music controllers. Anything that sends keyboard-mappable commands can be hijacked for use with Live – game controllers, joysticks and trackballs are all candidates. The Griffin Technology PowerMate (www.griffintechnology.com) is…hard to describe: imagine an enormous aluminium knob, that sits on your desk, and connects via USB to your laptop. It rotates like a knob, but also has a push button function. This was originally designed to act as a funky volume control, but has since become popular in all kinds of multimedia uses – it's good for scrubbing through timelines and selecting areas in a waveform. The PowerMate would be good for working with effects in real time, or perhaps in Ableton Live, for scrolling through scenes. And – I nearly forgot – it has a cute pulsating light at its base, so it would look good on a darkened stage too.

Griffin Technology PowerMate.

If you like the sound of that, then see also Contour Design's button-rich Shuttle range (www.contourdesign.com).

Contour Design Shuttle Pro.

QWERTY to MIDI

There is a way of adding a little more functionality to these things, a way that also makes them compatible with standard MIDI applications. Junxion (www.steim.org) is a utility which enables you to map any command from a qwerty keyboard/mouse/joystick/gamepad/etc to a specific MIDI function. Junxion used with one of the gadgets mentioned above, a joystick for example, would make an interesting MIDI controller. Junxion is Mac only, but Windows users can try either MIDI Joystick (http://members.magnet.at/hubwin/midi.html) or LiveSticks (http://homepage1.nifty.com/tomo_ya/livesticks-e.html).

OK – let's take it one step further. You could use Keyspan's Digital Media Remote (www.keyspan.com) infra red remote control with Junxion to control your MIDI apps from across the stage! Neato! But let's take it one step further again – the Digital Media Remote receiver will respond to commands sent from any JVC-compatible remote control, so you could use a JVC remote instead of the supplied Keyspan one – it would be more ergonomic, and would have more buttons than the standard Keyspan model. This is theory, you understand, I haven't tried it – but I don't see any reason why it would fail.

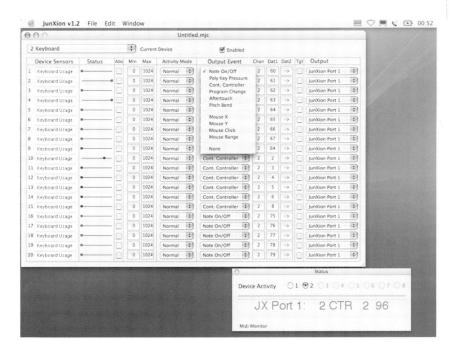

Junxion – assign MIDI functions to game controllers, mice, etc.

Accessories

Tumbling loosely into the bottom of our 'hardware' section, there are various smalls that need a quick mention before moving on.

Unless you plan to work solely from your laptop's speakers, headphones are required – use in-ear or folding types if you need to save space in your bag. Save your good headphones for special occasions – 'phones that live in your bag all day every day will take a pounding.

Another Ableton Live connection – the first time I saw the USB light (www.kensington.com) was when I was on the Ableton online store, ordering my original copy of Live. There it was, the USB light, with a little green 'Live' flag, and it seemed like the most obvious thing in the world. You'll find these all over the place now, like the USB version of a DJ's gooseneck lamp, in a variety of finishes, and with different coloured beams – there are ones with white, blue, and red lights.

Kensington USB light – great for low light conditions!.

How does it work? Simple – plug it into the USB port of your computer and it lights up. Bend it to the point where you want the light to go (onto the keyboard would seem the most likely option), and there you have it. This is my most-used accessory, I always have it on stage – especially handy because I work with the stage lights dimmed to emphasise my video projections. There are also fans(!) and webcams in the same flexy USB style.

• *If you've got a bronze G3, a USB light is not unnecessary when you're in a darkened DJ booth and you're trying to trigger Ableton samples off the keyboard! A while back we were on our way to a gig and we had a problem with the car. It started making this horrible noise – we didn't have a torch with us, so Simon just opened his laptop near the engine and we shone the USB light in and found the problem.* J-Lab

Info

Belkin do an add-on battery pack for the iPod, which will give 20 hours from four AA batteries.

Those iPods are so useful! Not being content with operating as an MP3/AAC/AIF/WAV player and hard drive, the iPod will now function as an audio recorder, with the addition of the Belkin iPod Voice Recorder (www.belkin.com). The recorder attaches to the iPod's remote/headphone connector, and includes a small (16mm) speaker. Hundreds of hours of audio can be recorded on an iPod; if you already travel with an iPod, this is a small addition which adds a big feature! Recorded material can then be transferred to your computer for editing/archiving via iTunes. The iPod is capable of playing and storing uncompressed audio at CD quality; however the Voice Recorder will only capture audio in mono, and at 16bit/8KHz, which is quite low resolution – although I still think this will be usable for certain sampling tasks.

You could successfully use the Voice Recorder to gather samples, move them to your computer for song building and mixing, then move the mixes back to the iPod for review. Although it's been promoted as a consumer product, the iPod gets more musician-friendly all the time. I can imagine somebody making a higher-spec front end for the iPod, that will add more recording functions at a higher resolution. Can't wait!

• *Don't waste your money on a ludicrously expensive mic; I use one of those little £5 computer mics that you can pick up in any computer shop – it's omnidirectional so great for acoustic environments, and so sensitive that you can get great recordings of even some insects with them. The other benefit of them is that they fit in your sleeve nicely with the wire just coming out of your bag, so you can record loads of things without people knowing it!* Ergo Phizmiz

If you want to use a mic preamp, then you'll need at least one microphone. I have a tendency to use whatever's available, I'm no expert in this field. I will say that you can get surprisingly good recordings with surprisingly bad mics, and that it's best to have a few to choose from. Then to go with the mic, you'll need some sort of small mic stand; I use those mini-tripods you get in photography shops; they're really versatile.

The samplist's friend, minidisc is the perfect way to get quite spontaneous good quality recordings. Team a minidisc recorder with a t-mic from Sony (www.sony.com) or the Sound Professionals (www.soundprofessionals.com), and you've got a mini recording setup that can't be beat – suddenly the world is just begging to be recorded. Street noise, machines, conversations, it's all fair game. Most people don't recognise a t-mic, so you can get away with recording in all kinds of situations – if you hold the minidisc recorder properly, people either don't notice it at all, or assume it's a mobile phone.

From kids' toys to keyrings shaped like microphones, to more 'serious' products, digital recorders are everywhere, and they are all usable, one way or another. Some are horribly crude, but they can be the most fun to use! Recordings made with cheap toy recorders are harsh and low resolution, but they can sound just right in the midst of a track produced with samples and sounds from other sources. They're also useful for re-recording something you've programmed, for example a drum loop, to give it a nasty edge. Use it instead of – or layered with – the original. Once you start moving upmarket, the choice is endless, from digital dictation recorders, to new creations like Creative Lab's MuVo (www.us.creative.com), essentially a USB storage device that doubles as an MP3 player with recording capabilities.

You're not going to carry them everywhere you go, but sometimes battery powered speakers are fun. They're no way good enough to mix on, in fact they often sound horrible. However, they're useful for doing presentations (if that's something you have to do), they're fun for jamming, and they're great for busking!

- *I haven't bought a USB fan – yet. There are also these USB fluorescent tube things which flash and change colour according to the beat , there's about three different designs for those too. Maybe that's what the 'U' in USB stands for – unnecessary. There's a lot of stuff around, and I look forward to there being more unnecessary gadgets. I like that I've got an Apple pen and an Apple keyring. I like all the stickers. I've got an Ableton Live t-shirt; I think those things are fun, they are blatantly toys sometimes, buts it's nice to have something fresh, it's like changing your desktop pattern, it makes it feel fresher…it's like that time once a year when you have to change your underwear.* mindlobster

Awkward question

Why make music with a laptop?

- *The laptop really is the ultimate appliance for electronic composers to perform live. There is nothing better as a performer than to be able to just jump on a train with your laptop and a few wires and just plug in to wherever you happen to be playing – unfortunately I tend to carry tubas and trombones and other massive and ridiculous objects to gigs, which kind of renders my last statement about convenience a little obsolete!* Ergo Phizmiz

- *It's really nice to be able to set up two, maybe even three to a table, and all be working on tracks, and then all be able to flip a laptop around, ask for each others' opinions, and be able to mess with it or change it.* Printz Board (musician, Black Eyed Peas Band)

Laptop computers used to be highly desirable, but mostly unaffordable, techno-lust objects toted about only by business types, 'high-end' professionals, and the more affluent geek.

Nowadays, while it's true that laptops are still out of reach of many people's wallets, they are a far more common sight. Take a ride on public transport – the tube, bus, train – in any city and you will see literally dozens of people carrying that give-away black padded case, encrusted with zippers. Laptops are here, and they've been kicking around long enough to have evolved into credible alternatives to desktop computers.

- *Convenience, speed and power. Laptops are more flexible, that rackful of synths can be simulated.*   Douglas Benford

- *I've recently joined a guitar band (playing with my laptop) and it's great because I don't have to drag a lot of gear around – I'm lazy...*   Pendle

Here's the formula: availability + high power = rock'n'roll.

- *All of this stuff is affordable and so functional, like the Oxygen8. That is the greatest thing ever. And that little backpack (Studiopack)? I would have paid double for those things. I take the Oxygen8 and work with that stuff almost everywhere. Now with PowerBooks, soft synths, the Oxygen8 and programs like Live and Reason, we can write anywhere. And we do write anywhere.*   Ken Jordan (musician, Crystal Method)

If you already have a laptop for work or study or internet or DVDs, then you might as well increase its workload and do some music on it. It might be the first time you've ever tinkered with music production, or it might be a supplement to a hefty studio set-up; either way, it's a shame to waste it!

- *If you do still think of composition and recording and performance as separate things, then I strongly suggest you think again, because there's no need for that any more. If you're writing at home on your laptop there's no reason why you cant take it out that night and perform with it and then you'll go home and see your composition in a different light as well. It gives you a great chance to try your 'works in progress' in front of an audience before you commit to anything. Music is a lot more fluid now – it's only when you finally burn it to CD that you'd call it finished.*   mindlobster

Music on a laptop means freedom to listen, write, record, and perform anywhere, no mains outlet required. If you get an idea for a sound, or a noise, or an entire song, wherever you are, you can start work on it now, and then take it home and polish it, burn it to disc or put it online or whatever, all on the same computer. This book was almost entirely written on the same laptop I record, compose, and perform with, in coffee shops, parks, and on trains – and any parts not written on the laptop were written on a PDA.

- *I can 'get out more' now. which was always the plan – to play and record and improvise with lots of interesting musicians.*   SongCarver

Maybe laptop music happens because of a desire by computer musicians to be liberated from the stuffy womb-like confines of the studio and desktop, a desire to – like 'proper' or 'traditional' musicians – take their instruments out into the world. Maybe it just happens because it can, because the technology is now available, and because it's kind of neat – that is reason enough.

People who use laptops are choosing to use 'worse' computers than similarly-priced desktop models. That's 'worse' in terms of screen acreage, processor power, memory, connectivity, etc., and laptop musicians are more likely to be pushing their computers to the limit. In the must-have-upgrade world of computers, CHOOSING to use fewer resources is distinctly odd, but if you're the kind of person who is excited by laptops, then you have different priorities.

- *I don't drive. I don't wanna haul round a load of synths everywhere, attractive though they can be with their winking lights and everything.* mindlobster

Laptops have only one thing going for them: portability. They get you out and about.

- *I started out restoring and performing analogue modular synths (Serge and Buchla models). They proved incredibly unreliable in live performance, so I switched to a computer to improve the reliability factor. It also took quite a weight off of the amount of gear we had to move.* Mochipet (performer)

- *It's all about portability. It allows me to work almost everywhere under all kinds of circumstances, and it saves me lots of time, because for playing live I just use the machine I used to compose my tracks, so there's no need to transfer files.* Eavesdropper

If portability is the only advantage, what is to be gained from this portability? A return to the stage; physical as opposed to virtual social interaction; you can work ad hoc in short bursts on location instead of in preordained blocks of several hours at a time.

- *Ease of transport. It is literally a portable studio. I use my laptop for performing my ambient music. Also, I bring my laptop over to my studio mate's house to jot down ideas for our studio tracks.* JDG

- *To be able to take my laptop on the road with me allows for me to work anywhere.* Neil Wiernik

A lot of music software products are sold on their ability to emulate or replace 'real' hardware, although thankfully this is changing – good software should exist in its own right, not as a cheap alternative to something else, and the software that should be most interesting to 'modern' computer musicians is not the software that apes hardware, but the software that goes in a totally new direction, providing new sounds or new working methods or both.

Some people say hardware is better (you usually hear this argument in terms of synthesiser nostalgia), while others have abandoned hardware altogether, and rely on soft synths, samplers, and sequencers for everything. And gadget fiends who are into laptops don't have to go without their hardware fix – there is a world of hardware audio and MIDI interfaces out there, not to mention the MIDI control surfaces and keyboard controllers.

Joe Youg – laptop composer, in his own words

I use a G3/400 Mac PowerBook (very old school now). I abandoned my hardware three years ago, and now use virtual instruments when I need them, and samples from all sorts of sources and recordings.

I have an M-Audio Duo USB audio interface, a portable minidisc recorder for field recordings and an Oxygen8 keyboard – that's about it for hardware.

Software (still running on OS9) is Opcode Studio Vision for MIDI work, with Reason running as a slave via the IAC bus – this provides all my basic sounds. I then take a stereo mix into radiaL where I subject composed fragments to intense processing and time-stretching and save these results as stereo files. These are finally taken into Pro Tools Free for collaging and assembly into the final pieces.

Joe Young is a composer whose working methods have been transformed by his use of laptop computers.

The uniqueness of my approach lies in the type of sounds that I use for this work, and how I source them. In addition to the usual approach of plundering my record collection for sounds/loops, which are then transformed beyond the point of recognition, I use the minidisc to capture improvisations from the actors I'm working with, and use these as a further element in my sound palette.

My background is as an actor, and it is through this understanding of the effect that music has on performance that I sculpt my work. My compositions sit on the edge of music and sound design and it was this particular angle that interested radio producer Karen Rose – I will therefore be processing some of the sound effects on their Pro Tools system as part of my compositional role. This is a fairly unusual crossing of job specs, and myself and the recording engineer have yet to work out exactly where his job finishes and mine begins!

I aim to capture a mood that comes from the text – and I always make sure that the music has a direct connection to the historical period of the piece, either through quotation or implication. I try to avoid pastiche of existing musical styles, although the resulting soundtrack may travel through various musical forms. For 'Full Blown' I decided on processed piano plus suggestions of water and hospital machinery – the music was linked into William Blake poetry that is quoted during the play, but never actually accompanies the poetry. What it hopefully does is glue the various elements of the writing together.

It's the ability to work anywhere that led me to working with a laptop in the first place. I can take rough sketches into rehearsal and compose on the fly with radiaL. It works like an instrument, rather than a sample playback device, and the control that I have over audio is much more than is possible using a simple sampler and sequencer combo.

I am based mostly in the Theatre and Beyond office (www.theplaysthething.com) and much of my theatre work happens now with them. I tend to work independently and after having initial meetings with the director/producer, I'm pretty much left to get on with it.

Doing it ... with software

* *The laptop is an Instrument which does not have any inbuilt sound.* Slender Whiteman

* The beauty of software on the laptop is you can break out of any working regime and try new things. It keeps things fresh. J-Lab

The world is full of software. There's more music software out there than anybody could ever need, with so much crossover, duplication and redundancy...the wheel is reinvented on a daily basis...somebody will try to tell you that their wheel is better, rounder, than that bumpy old wheel you're struggling along with now. And very little of that software is laptop-specific. The intention of this book isn't to repeat a lot of general information about computer music; it's about looking at things from a laptop user's POV.

Editors

You will need to edit audio at some point. Editing audio for laptop users is pretty much the same as for desktop users, except your computer is likely to max out sooner when you start doing too many things at once.

Editors can be free and they can be expensive; they all have their own spin on things, they all add different features to the basic editing functions, so you have to decide what works best for you – if you're seriously into sampling, it could be that you spend a lot of time working with an editor, so you better get one that does what you want in a way that you're happy with.

Ableton Live doesn't offer any editing features at all, but it does have a convenient shortcut button — when you have a clip selected in Live, click on the 'edit' button in the 'clip view' window, and the sample will be opened in the editor that you've specified in Live's preferences. This is essential — although Live will let you select portions of a sound file to use as a clip, it doesn't shed the surplus, so you can end up with a lot of space-wasting audio junk on your drive.

Editors are also useful because they're very fast to set up for recording — if you're out somewhere working on your laptop and you quickly want to record something that's going on with your built-in mic, it's usually faster to prepare an editor for recording than a sequencer.

- *The minimum software you need is an audio editor — which you can hopefully record into as well as just open and edit files — and some sort of performance tool, so obviously being a Live user I'm going to say everybody should have Ableton Live. You don't need anything else.* mindlobster

Audacity

The good news about editors is that you don't need to spend a lot of money to get one (and I'm not talking about your mate's prehistoric pirated copy of SoundEdit). Audacity (http://audacity.sourceforge.net) is a good place to start. It's well-specified, totally cross platform (Windows 98 – XP, Mac OSX, Linux), open source, and free (although donations are gratefully accepted). Most editors that are free or cheap versions of 'pro' apps have some restrictions or limitations, but Audacity does its best to cover all the bases; there's no limit on the length or number of tracks you can have in a project (except your computer's ability to handle them); and it's claimed that Audacity will 'import almost anything', including WAV, AIFF,

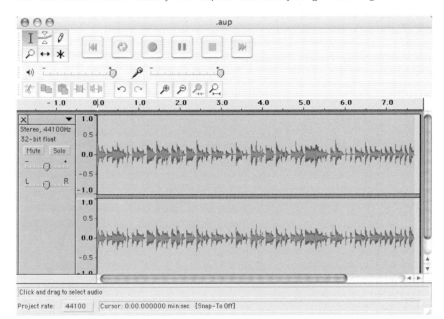

Audacity — free cross-platform audio editor.

Next/AU, IRCAM, MP3 and Ogg Vorbis (though not directly from an audio CD) – furthermore the 'Import Raw Data' feature attempts to identify any file format you throw at it – I have a lot of fun listening to the noises it makes when playing imported images or text files. Imported audio can be viewed as usual in waveforms, or as spectrograms.

Once you've got it imported or recorded, audio can be edited (with unlimited undo's), and treated with the supplied effects, including compressor, phaser, reverb and noise removal, or with VST, LADSPA, or Nyquist plug-ins (Nyquist is a DIY programming language that uses files created in text editors).

MIDI files can be imported and viewed, though this is pretty pointless, as they can't be played or edited at present; I assume these features will be added in future (perhaps by the time you read this). I appreciated the labelling feature: labels can be inserted at any point on the timeline – notes about the audio, or transcriptions of speech – and exported later as a text file, with the exact start time at the beginning of each label. If you need to make a lot of labels, extra label tracks can be added. Audacity also supports keyboard shortcuts for commonly-used instructions. When you've finished working on your sounds, Audacity can export them in AIFF, WAV, Sun/Next, and Ogg Vorbis.

If you've just downloaded Audacity, you'll find that it won't let you export files as MP3s – this is because MP3 encoders are supposed to be licensed from the Fraunhofer Institute – not popular amongst the open source community! However, third-party encoding plug-ins such as LAME can be downloaded and added to Audacity – see the Audacity website for more info.

Even if you're already using another editor, Audacity is worth a look. It might have features that your current editor doesn't – who said you have to stick with just one? The interface is unsophisticated, but unlike most open source apps, the design is functional and successful, without any of the idiosyncratic twists and graphical anomalies that plague Linux audio apps. Audacity is a viable alternative to piracy for the underfunded musician, and a viable alternative to spending money for everybody else.

Why pay more? It leaves you with disposable cash for joysticks, interfaces – or maybe even taking a loved one out for dinner.

Open source Audacity (quoted from the website)

Audacity was started in the fall of 1999 by Dominic Mazzoni while he was a graduate student at Carnegie Mellon University in Pittsburgh, PA, USA. He was working on a research project with his advisor, Professor Roger Dannenberg, and they needed a tool that would let them visualise audio analysis algorithms. Over time, this program developed into a general audio editor, and other people started helping out.

Today, Audacity is developed using Sourceforge, an online site that allows people around the world to collaborate on free software projects. See sourceforge.net for more information. Dozens of people have contributed to Audacity, and progress is continually accelerating.

Record your laptop's output

This is a very crude method I sometimes use to record my laptop's speaker output without using any other hardware. I originally used it to record my Mac's text-to-speech, which is now redundant because I can use WireTap (www.ambrosia.com), which will record any audio output by the Mac's system, but it's still fun for crude 'resampling'/'degrading' effects. If you're trying it with Audacity, open Audacity first, then open the file that you want to play back (in whatever application). Make sure your system volume is at max and your built-in mic is selected as the recording source, then start recording in Audacity, and start playback of the file you want to re-record. That's it – this works with most recording apps *but* you *must* make sure that any 'record monitor' options are disabled, otherwise you may get some nasty feedback!

TC Works' Spark ME (www.tcelectronic.com, demos available) is another high quality free editor – Mac-only – but with a far slicker interface than Audacity's. If you do get the urge to spend money on an editor, remember that Spark ME is but the base version of the range, increasing in complexity, features, and price. Other popular commercial editors include the Windows-only Sound Forge (www.sound-forge.com, save disabled demo available), and another Mac-only app, Peak (www.bias-inc.com, fully working 14 day demo available), and the application formerly known as Cool Edit, Adobe Audition (www.adobe.com, time-limited demo).

Before you spend money on an editor, download some demos, and try living with one of the free ones for a while. You might find that the free ones do everything you want, or you might discover a 'can't live without it' feature in one of the commercial editors. It's a personal thing; I've been using Spark LE for a while, which is the cheapest upgrade from Spark ME, but more recently I've started using Audacity as well.

Spark LE screen - note this is the LE not ME version.

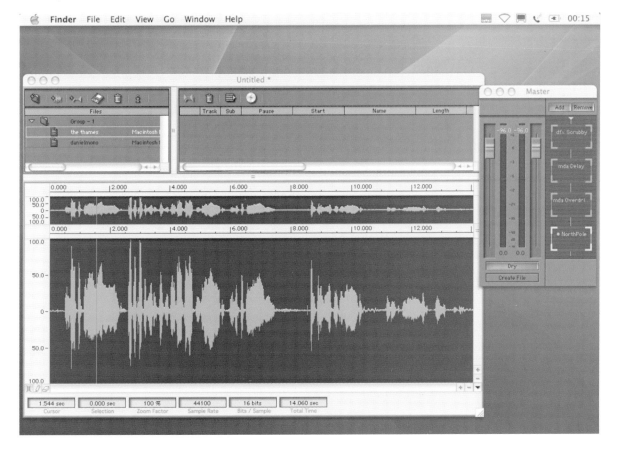

Jamming with editors

You can have fun jamming with a simple editor. With a stereo editor like Audacity or Spark LE, for example, you can apply up to four plug-ins to a piece of audio, and then move between them, tweaking their parameters in real time as you go. With a sequencer such as Metro (www.sagantech.biz) this can be done with several tracks at once. It's not the same kind of jamming/performance experience you get with an application like Ableton Live or radiaL, but it's still a lot of fun, and it might lead to some interesting results.

Sequencers

Laptop music is a different way of doing things, and using the same old sequencers isn't necessarily the best way to go. There is software now that subtly bends the rules, puts a new slant on old concepts, and there is software that throws the rule book away entirely. Cubase and Logic and Pro Tools are all valid apps, and they can have their place in a laptop based set-up, but they are not (here it comes again) laptop-specific, and besides, there are newer arrivals and newer perspectives, from less established companies, that are worth looking at.

REplayPLAYer

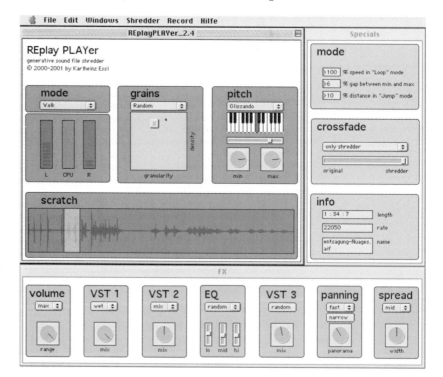

Quote

I use very basic versions of Logic, and editing software Soundmaker, but the backbone to a lot of my material lately is some generative software called REplayPLAYer (www.essl.at/works/ replay.html), which I process a lot of my sounds in.
Douglas Benford

Ableton Live

Of these more 'recent' developments, the most obvious is Ableton Live (www.able-ton.com). Is it a sequencer? Is it a sampler? Is it a performance tool? Well...yes. No matter how you choose to categorise or separate the activities of composition, recording and performance, Live insinuates itself into all of them. Whatever you're doing with your laptop – whatever kind of music, and wherever you're doing it – you should be using Live.

If Live wasn't designed exclusively for laptop use, it might as well been. It was conceived and developed by Robert Henke and Gerhard Behles (aka German electronic duo Monolake), when they needed performance software that would lend itself to improvisation rather than the timeline-based working methods of existing applications. There are legions of users who had never considered performing on stage with a laptop until Live came along; before Live appeared I was on stage with hardware sequencers and samplers, and laptop jamming with QuickTime Pro and Metro.

- *Software sequencers and hard-disk recording applications were originally designed as studio tools, replacing tape machines. Historically, they were more aimed towards sound engineers than towards musicians. The underlying idea of timeline-based editing is construction and sculpturing, not so much performing. As a result, those tools fail onstage or in any context where improvisation or interaction with musicians is essential. So all the software Gerhard and I wrote for our own purposes enabled us to interact with the music in real time. We liked the concept of step sequencers and drum computers because they allowed for immediate control of structure by changing patterns in real time. Live is the result of applying some of these ideas to the world of sound files, thus providing more flexibility and easy access to an infinite pool of possible source material.* Robert Henke (aka Monolake, performer and co-creator of Ableton Live)

Ableton call Live a 'sequencing instrument'. It's one of the few apps that creates a situation, a vibe, where the laptop starts to feel like an instrument in its own right. It's an instrument that makes no sound of its own, however; in that respect, Live is more like a sampler – sounds must be recorded or imported into it.

Live is cross-platform – it works with Mac OSX, and Windows 98/2000/XP. The interface is incredibly laptop-friendly, for situations where screen space is in short supply. It can run in full-screen mode, and individual features such as the mixer and file browser can be concealed/revealed with keyboard shortcuts, enabling you to manipulate the display according to what you need at any moment during your session/gig/jam. Unlike certain other apps which strive to emulate hardware's traditions, Live keeps virtual knobs and faders to a minimum – the interface is easy to grasp, whether you've used music software before or not (one of the things that makes Live great for educational purposes), and if you do have problems with it then the Info View window will be your friend and tell you what you're rolling over!

- *If I ever see another pair of rack ears again it will be too soon, Live is the ultimate tool for me. So far I'm just working with Live on drums and percussion. It's my drummer and percussionist here at home or for working on my stuff on the road, and I record my electric piano parts from the Emagic EVP88 virtual piano instrument and my sax live into Logic running alongside it. Like everyone, I have a lot of loops at various tempos and pitches and I've always had to contour the tempos of my tunes to accommodate the tempo of each. That problem is eliminated by Live—just toss a loop into it and tell it what tempo you want to play in. The mic stand is by far the hardest thing for me to pack when I travel. I could take a smaller suitcase if there was a telescoping mic stand out there somewhere.* Tom Scott (jazz musician)

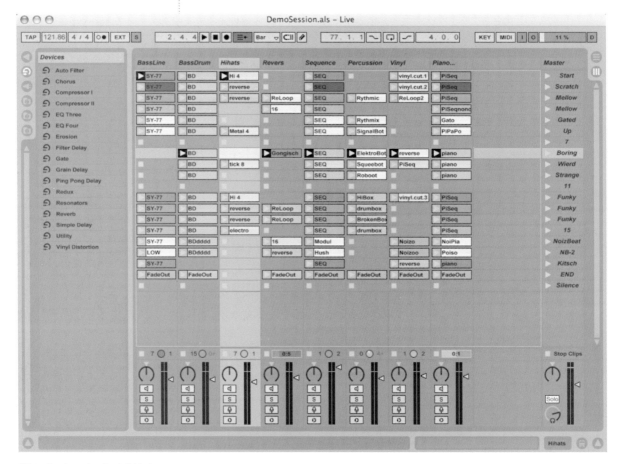

Ableton Live. In session view individual sound clips can be triggered, tweaked, and processed in real time.

All activities in Live concern two 'views' – the session view, where individual sound clips can be triggered, tweaked, and processed in real time, or bunches of clips called 'scenes' can be triggered simultaneously, and the arrange view, where a more considered sequencing type approach can be used. In reality however, the distinctions between these views are minimal. If you use Live's record feature while jamming in the session view, then the resulting 'recording' can be viewed and edited in the arrange view. Furthermore, you can use the session view to jam over a piece that you've done in the arrange view; there is a constant interplay between the two different views. The arrange and session views are supplemented by a browser window, from where you can drag'n'drop effects (proprietary Live ones and third party VST), and from where you can search for and preview audio files, and mixer, in/out, sends, overview and clip windows. Keyboard shortcuts can be used to navigate between, or conceal/reveal these windows on demand, without interrupting playback.

- *I have used Ableton Live for a very long time now. When I bought it I did not know what to use it for exactly. First I found that I liked to use it as a luxurious loop editor, ReWire-slaved in Cubase. With Live, it was so easy and fast to try out various loops with my Cubase arrangement. Everything fit together; categories like Techno, Trance and House did not seem to matter anymore.*

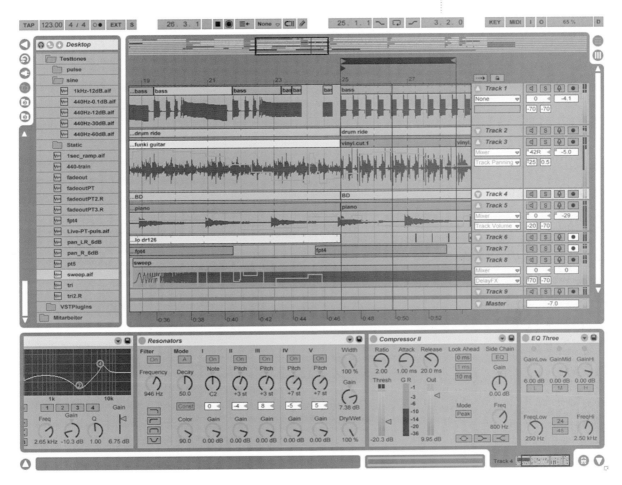

Ableton Live arrange view.

Speed differences of 30 bpm did not create audible problems – and pitching whole tracks over three semitones still sounded great. When I found out about the possibility of syncing a whole track by using Live´s Warp Markers, I immediately loaded about 150 songs onto my G4, warp-marked them and tried to find matching combinations. Mijk Van Dijk (DJ)

- *You can just throw a few samples together in a hurry with Live, create an arrangement and just see where it takes you. The audio engine takes care of tempo corrections. Composing becomes so intuitive, you can hear immediately if it works or not. With traditional software it usually takes a lot longer, and it takes hours to tweak the tempo.* DJ Rabuake (DJ, what else?)

Most of Live's features can be assigned to a qwerty key and/or a MIDI controller; this is easier to do in Live than in any other application I've tried. To assign a qwerty key: command/k, and all assignable controls will be highlighted. Click on the one you want to assign, and then press the qwerty key you want to use. Repeat the process for subsequent assignments, then command/k when you've finished (you can't assign two functions to the same key – though sometimes that would be useful). That's it. MIDI works the same way – command/m, click on the control you want to assign, then hit the knob/fader/button on your MIDI hardware. When you've gone to the trouble of setting these controls up, you can make them the default settings using the 'save template' option, so that next time you launch Live all your favourite qwerty/MIDI controls will be there. One of Live's most useful features in work flow terms is the ability to quickly map one sample across a MIDI keyboard without it creating a lot of screen-hogging individual clips.

- *Basically, I think of Live as a drum machine. It's as simple to operate as a can of soda. It works all day long and it will not crash. Certainly I do complete performances on it, but I am always recording its output as though it were a performance instrument, which I then record on my multitrack, which just happens to be another computer.* Charlie Clouser (musician/producer)

As well as drag'n'drop from folders, Live can record directly from your audio interface, on single or multiple tracks. You can even go online and download samples from within Live during your set (that's if you can get online at the venue).

Once your sounds are in Live, it quickly starts to show what it's capable of. Not only can any sound (or section of a sound) be treated in the usual sampler ways – looping, one-shots, etc – by using Live's warp markers, a sound's timing can be manipulated: its rhythmic nature can be edited to fit in with the other parts of your song. It's called elastic audio – it means you can start to treat audio in the same way as MIDI files – a vocal or a drum loop can have its rhythm, pitch, and duration completely changed. Even better, these changes can be made in real-time, while your song is playing, so what might in one situation be 'editing' becomes 'performance' in another.

Live clip info window.

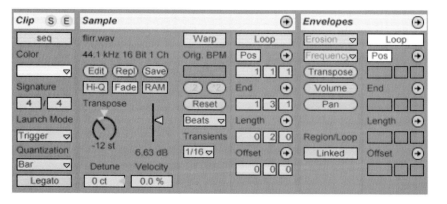

- *I used to use Live for more experimental stuff, and Reason for more straight-forward dance floor stuff, but now I've got so into Live and its possibilities I'm using it for dance floor stuff as well. I like the danger of 'okay where am I going to take it now?', but I've got to keep everybody dancing. It's like being in a band again.* J-Lab

As with sound clips, effects can be dropped into your set and tweaked in real time, so nothing has to interrupt your flow. If your computer struggles under all those plug-ins you've just dropped into your drum track, then you can bounce Live's output to a new track, or render a part to disk then reimport it, to reduce the load.

The arrange view offers a reasonable amount of control over automation too, as the performance tool becomes the sequencer. It's good to be able to do all these functions in one app – although there are benefits in using 'specialised' applications for each task, there is a fluidity which can only be got this way.

And finally, when your masterpiece is complete, the whole can be mixed down to a stereo file, and the project can be saved in a self-contained form, copying all of the used audio files to a single location for easy archiving.

Live info clips

If you've got a lot going on in your Live set, create a silent clip by importing a very short silent AIF/WAV, and then use the clip name function to put some info in the area of the clip. Obviously there isn't a lot of room, but even short notes to yourself like '140 BPM' or 'CHAN 3' (meaning send channel change 3 from the MIDI keyboard here), can be really useful. Of course the 'info' clips can also be colour coded for extra significance. Some people, when performing a set using Live, pause between songs to open a new Live file for each song. I prefer to have my entire set in one file; that way I can make smooth transitions between songs. Once you have that much material on screen, some form of labelling becomes even more useful.

At one level all you need to rock'n'roll is a copy of Live, and a laptop with a built-in mic. At the other extreme you can use Live on stage with a band of 'traditional' instruments, or in a studio with assorted hardware and software.

Live is made for laptops; I don't know if it was *actually* made for laptops, but it's the most laptop-friendly music app around, with its easily manipulated interface and qwerty control. Of course it can be run on a desktop computer, but somehow that seems to be against the point. Live is more like a lifestyle product than a typical piece of music software – literally a life-changing experience (in a musical sense); no wonder users develop strangely proprietary feelings towards it.

Live will be a hard act to follow, for Ableton and their competition – they got it beautifully right first time out. I don't know what they have planned for the future; in a way I hope it doesn't change too much – it could be a tough exercise to add more features without compromising the interface.

Download the demo and try it. Or just cut out the middle man and buy it straight away; you won't be sorry.

- *For someone who's a musician, getting into computers and wants to express their musicality, maybe Reason's a good one because you've got synthesisers and it's MIDI-able, and you can play it from a keyboard. If it's someone who's just getting into music and has no formal training and wants to get something happening, I suppose Ableton Live is a good one to go for.* J-Lab

There are also 'lite' versions of Live that you'll run into from time to time, usually bundled with hardware such as Mackie's Spike or M-Audio's FireWire 410. There's also something called Remix, from Steinberg (www.steinberg.com), which is a very cheap version of Live, licensed from Ableton. It lacks many of Live's most important features, but as I said it is cheap, so you'll have to have a little talk with your wallet. Remix's limitations include: no Rewire, no audio in, eight track limit, sixteen scene limit, only five built-in effects, only one VST available at once, and no qwerty keyboard assignments.

Quote

The app doesn't do it for you! It's what we call Photoshop music – where people throw together a bunch of sounds and it just sounds generic. IriXx

Propellerheads' Reason

Live must be one of the most commonly-found apps on music laptops, and one of the *other* most common is Propellerheads' Reason (www.propellerheads.com). Philosophically though, Reason is at the other end of the spectrum from Live – it does all it can to replicate the look of classic hardware, with its virtual rack which can be rotated to view the virtual cables at the rear, complete with animated virtual swaying (thankfully this can be turned off).

There is a fair selection of devices to add to Reason's virtual rack – Mixer, SubTractor Analog Synth, Malstrom Graintable Synth, NN19 Sampler, NNXT sampler, Dr Rex Loop Player, Redrum Drum Computer, Matrix Pattern Sequencer, Spider Audio and CV Merger/Splitters, RV7000 Advanced Reverb, Scream 4 Distortion, BV512 Digital Vocoder, RV7 Reverb, DDL1 Delay, D11 Distortion, ECF42 Envelope Controlled Filter, CF101 Chorus/Flanger, PH90 Phaser, UN16 Unison, Comp 01 Compressor/Limiter, and the PEQ2 Two Band EQ. That's a lot of virtual hardware – there's no limit on how many instances of a particular device can be in one rack, and the routing options add even more flexibility and potential to the setup. This might be time to mention that Reason is a very closed system – there are no third party plug-ins or extra devices available. Furthermore, at the moment Reason has no audio recording functions – though this could of course change in the future!

The other major Reason component is the sequencer, which can appear in the bottom of the rack, or be separated and opened across your display – which puts it in a much more usable position. This helps a lot when it comes to managing screen space – one of the irrationalities of Reason's vertically scrolling rack design is the poor way it adapts to the horizontally-biased layout of computer screens. Once you pop out the sequencer window and start viewing the rack as a container for your instruments and effects, you can treat Reason more like a traditional sequencer – although

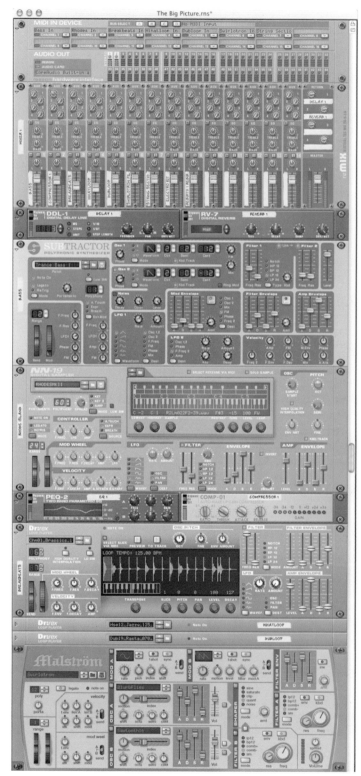

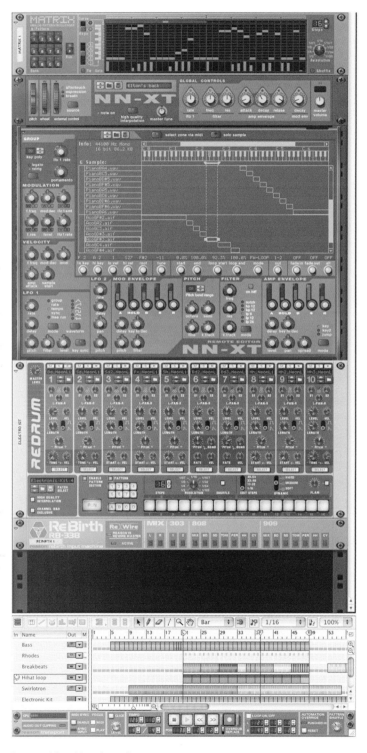

Reason rack front (shown here split over two pages).

there are far better sequencers out there, Reason's neat all-in-one coherence is strongly in its favour.

Adding a MIDI keyboard/controller to Reason is highly recommended, especially if you want to use the linear sequencer functions rather than the pattern based programming options. Although not as simple as with Live, it's relatively easy to assign MIDI controllers to Reason's devices. Once the setup's been done, working with Reason becomes more spontaneous, and of course being able to play the instrument sounds from a keyboard is more rewarding then working exclusively with the pattern-based Matrix sequencer.

One problem I've always had with Reason is that there seems to be a certain, shall we say, generic quality to songs that are produced solely within the virtual rack. Reason users need to be working at quite a high level before their individuality can come across. The demo songs that are supplied with Reason don't help to dispel this idea; I really think that Propellerheads need to try harder to find more varied demo material. The pattern-based method of composition also seems to lead people down certain familiar paths. Perhaps that's why the Orkester strings content CD is included, to point people in a different direction?

The more sounds of your own you add, whether in the Redrum kits, or in the NN samplers, the better your chances of having a distinctive sound. The Reload application, which is a free download from the Propellerheads site for registered users, is a tool which can help differentiate you from the standard Reason sounds – it's a utility that creates Reason Refills (a compressed 'bundle' of formatted sounds) from Akai format CDs. Being able to use my Akai sounds in Reason made it a lot more interesting to me. The NNXT sampler also opens sound font files, many of which are available on the internet, some free, some commercial.

Propellerheads try hard to persuade you not to use pirate copies of Reason. The packaging is gorgeous, there's a good printed manual, and registered users can download extra content from the website. Reason's popularity also means that there are many Refills available, some of which are free – see the Propellerheads site for links, and try www.reason2refill.com.

What Reason most has going for it is convenience – the no-mess self-contained structure is very attractive, if you're getting tired of endless VSTs and soft synths knocking against each other in your sequencer. I don't think Reason sounds as good as some other synth apps – this is a subjective opinion, and I'm not a synth expert by any means, but I find the sounds in Unity Session, for example, much fuller and more usable (though Reason is more stable). I might sound like I'm on a downer with Reason – some days that is true, but I must say that I do use Reason frequently; always routed through Ableton Live via Rewire!

Akai format CDs and Reason

You can use the Reload application (available free to registered users from www.propellerheads.com) to convert your 'legacy' Akai programs and samples into the Refill format supported by Reason (or into Wav files for use in other audio applications); where applicable, keyboard mappings are supported. The ability to smoothly incorporate Akai material in this way is one of the things that begins to make Reason more 'usable'.

Download the demo from the website. You could also look at Reason Adapted, a simplified version available from Propellerheads, which I think also forms the basis of the branded version of Reason included in various software bundles.

Reason's stereo output as seen by Ableton Live when they are Rewired together.

Rewiring Reason and Ableton Live
Reason has limited audio recording and manipulation options, and somewhat incomplete sequencing functions, whereas Ableton Live makes no sounds of its own – when used together, they make a tasty app sandwich, with Rewire as the filling – or should that be the topping? Rewire was developed by Steinberg to enable music apps to sync together, and send audio to each other. If you use Rewire you can can apply VST plug-ins hosted by Live to Reason's outputs in real time. if you're going to use Reason with Live all the time, you don't even need to have a mixer in your Reason rack, just hardwire from Reason's 'hardware interface'. Instead of mucking around with Reason's sequencer, it's faster and adds a different dimension if you quickly grab chunks of Reason's output into Live and start treating them as samples immediately. You can capture the whole of Reason's stereo master output on one Live stereo track, or send different Reason instruments to their own Live tracks for individual enhancement/abuse.

Arturia Storm
If you're interested in Reason and the self-contained studio concept, then maybe you should take a look at Arturia's Storm (www.arturia.com). Frankly, I found Storm to be very Reasonesque, but just different enough to be confusing to use. It seems to be aimed at quite a different market from Reason – it's cheaper, and somehow less attractive for serious users, with its composition wizards for different styles of music, maximum of four instruments at a time, and blatantly trading on its being like a 'real' studio but 'for less money'.

There is one thing that Storm has over Reason, however – audio recording! Storm will record audio directly into its EZtrack module...maybe Propellerheads need to ask Arturia for a few tips. Like Reason, Storm supports Rewire, which might help overcome some of its drawbacks – for instance Arturia state that two instances of Storm can be active at once and Rewired together, but I couldn't try it because there was no OSX support at time of writing.

There'll be somebody out there who loves Storm, but I just couldn't get into it – it'll be easier to use if you haven't already tried Reason. If I was starting out and this had come along, I would have thought it was cool, though.

Tracktion

What with all this talk about 'elastic audio' and 'self-contained virtual studios' you might be thinking that the 'traditional' sequencer is on its way out. But this is where Raw Material Software's Tracktion comes in (www.rawmaterialsoftware.com). This is a new audio/MIDI sequencer for Mac, Windows, and (soon) Linux, which supports audio and MIDI recording, VSTs, and VSTis. Tracktion is good news for anybody (like me) who finds the established sequencers to be ungainly behemoths rather than musicians' tools, and if you're not tied to a legacy of Cubase or Logic projects then you should try it – the website tells us that Tracktion is 'kicking the audio football through the goalposts of usability". Excellent!

Launching Tracktion takes you to the Projects page – a 'project' is a collection of files, including sound files, MIDI files, and 'edits'. An edit is the particular collection of files within that project that relate to one piece of music – in other words, an edit is what you click to open when you want to work on a song and see the Tracktion sequencer window. Projects can be saved in self-contained archives, similar to the ones that Live uses, or they can be compressed at various quality ratios (using Ogg Vorbis files) if you want to make smaller bundles.

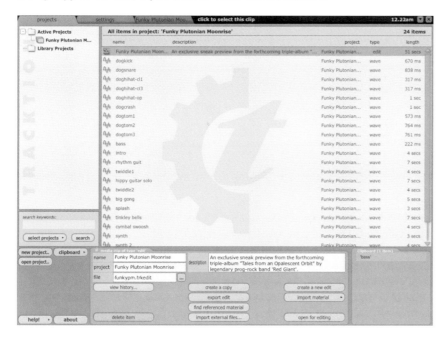

Tracktion Projects page.

The Tracktion interface is... well, it's quite Native Instruments in its colour scheme, and it has enormous rollover help balloons, which initially tend to obscure the interface, but can be reined in for more sensible viewing. Raw Material have taken the option of creating a menu-free full-screen interface, which avoids the need to accommodate OS-specific menu issues, but in losing that familiarity, forces users to figure out where everything is. Working in full screen is appreciated sometimes (it was good news when Live added it as an option), but that's what it should be – an option. It makes things especially difficult when you're using Tracktion to Rewire with another app, because you can't get em both on screen at the same time.

Tracktion Sequencer page.

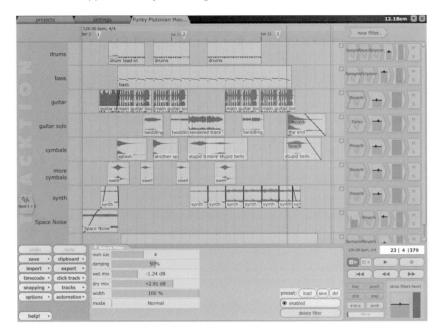

Tracktion is very accommodating when it comes to making connections. MIDI and audio interface setup is easy, and VSTs and VSTis were successfully identified. On the software side I tried it with various synths, samplers, and plug-ins including Unity Session, HALion, Crystal, MDA, and DFX; on the hardware side with the Oxygen8 and the FireWire 410 – with the latter successfully identifying its four inputs and 8 outputs.

Tracktion has many typical sequencer functions, including MIDI recording and editing, plug-in parameter automation, timestretching...it also has a 'track freeze' mode, where plug-in heavy tracks can be temporarily rendered for smoother play-back. With Tracktion, though, it's not so much about the functions as the interface, and, to be blunt, the price. Tracktion busts convention by being well-specified, well-designed, AND cheap. Even if you just bought to add improved sequencing and VSTi functions to apps like Reason or Live via Rewire, it would be worth it, and if you don't need any of the extra features provided by those apps, then Tracktion works very well on its own. There are demo versions for Mac and PC available on the website, and you might be interested to know that Tracktion is also included in the bundle with Mackie's Spike USB audio interface.

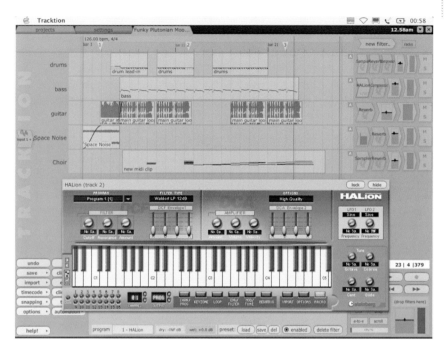

Tracktion and Halion.

Rewiring Tracktion and Live

Tracktion and Ableton Live can make a good combination. Live doesn't have any sort of MIDI sequencing or VSTi capabilities, and some people find Live's arrange view difficult to get to grips with. Here's how to set them up via Rewire:

1   Start Tracktion and open an edit.

2   Drag a new filter into the track where you want Live's audio output to appear, and choose Rewire device from the popup menu.

3   In the properties panel at the bottom of the screen, click 'choose device' and select Ableton Live from the popup menu.

4   Launch Live (at present it can't be launched from within Tracktion) – Live will display a message stating that Rewire master functions aren't available.

5   Start a clip or scene playing in Live, and you should get the audio output in Tracktion (you can either use Live's stereo master output, or separate buses for each track). Clicking 'start' in either app will begin them playing, but you must make tempo changes in Live not Tracktion. Now you can use Live's output alongside Tracktion's audio and MIDI functions, including VSTi parts. Disclaimer: tested on Mac OSX with a Beta version of Tracktion – this is how it worked for me, you might find things have changed slightly. Now I've discussed how to Rewire Tracktion with Live, and Live with Reason – as far as other Rewire-compatible apps go, the process should be pretty familiar. If for instance you find Reason's sequencer lacking in charm, then you can use Rewire to get Tracktion to do all the sequencing work. Rewire is incredibly useful when you have two apps which each seem to be 'missing something', and it's easy to set up.

Tracktion might be described as a sequencer for people who don't like sequencers – it's a viable alternative, not just something different for the sake of it.

Metro

Mac users who have reasons for avoiding Logic or Cubase or Digital Performer can also try Metro (www.sagantech.biz), which originated in the 1980s as a MIDI sequencer and has gradually evolved into a respectable MIDI/audio sequencer with support for VSTs, VSTis and Audio Units, and now includes a certain level of video editing.

I used to use Metro a lot in OS9 days. I could understand the interface (unlike some software sequencers), the price was right, it would open QuickTime movies, and (most important) it would run on my Bondi iMac without needing any kind of irritating dongle protection – that was important in those days of early USB (ie the late 90s). I stopped using Metro when I moved to OSX; I didn't really think Metro would make the leap, but I was wrong. Although, like its better known rivals, Metro has been through a lot of changes during its lifetime, its interface remains accessible, and setting up the application is much easier in these days of Coreaudio under OSX.

Metro's graphic editor is a powerful tool for MIDI editing, and it's possible to view MIDI, audio and video data simultaneously in the timeline. For those who crave a hardware-type experience, there's also a MIDI event editor window, with loooong editable lists of note and controller info. There are also a couple of interesting non-standard composition tools: the Rhythm Explorer and the Note Spray Paint Tool can be used to enter a (definable) random element to your sequencing.

'Proper' musicians will be interested in the notation window; parts can be built from scratch in this window, or MIDI files can be imported and edited. Up to 64 audio tracks can be used, and audio editing features are as refined as those on the MIDI side; time stretching was recently added. Audio support is now available up to 96KHz/32bit resolutions.

VSTs and AudioUnits can be used together, chained in the same track if required,

Metro's graphic editor is a powerful tool for MIDI editing.

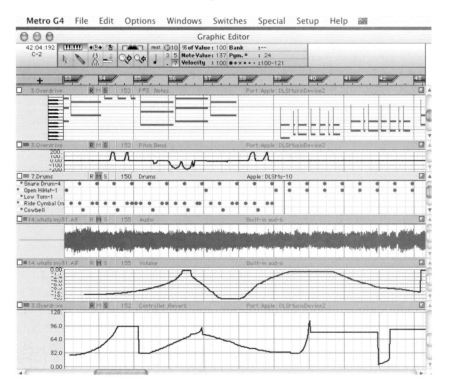

and all effects can be automated. Plug-in parameters can be controlled via MIDI from external hardware controllers, as can many other Metro functions. Any VSTi parts will be rendered as audio files alongside the rest of your song. Completed Metro projects can be saved as self-contained bundles for archiving or moving between computers.

Although basic, Metro's video capture and editing facilities are useful, especially if you want to work on a soundtrack while viewing (and if necessary editing) the movie at the same time. A few basic but handy filters and image adjustments are available, based on the standard QuickTime tools. Metro imports movie files from disk, or will capture from an attached camera – I have used it with a FireWire webcam, and it will capture time lapse images.

MIDI composition isn't what it was – it's a lot easier to work with audio these days as computers have become more powerful, but it is still necessary if you want to work with software instruments that aren't just pattern-based. If you do still work that way, or if you have an archive of old MIDI files that you want to continue working with, Metro is a realistically-priced and well-equipped solution. I've even used Metro as a jamming tool, using the realtime control over plug-ins and a few simple loops. The worse thing I can think of to say about Metro is that it lacks Rewire support; I wish they would add that because Rewire is becoming essential these days!

There's not enough space to cover Metro properly – go to the website and download the save-disabled demo; I should point out that there is also a slightly-simplified 'SE' version available.

Other sequencers that aren't Cubase or Logic

Quick mentions for other sequencers/compositional apps: Bitheadz Phrazer (www.bitheadz.com) is an audio composition sequencer from the people who brought us Unity Session (seen elsewhere in this book) – the recent version of Phrazer is much improved in terms of stability and accessibility, and features 900MB of quality sample content from Bitheadz sound libraries, and a further 480MB of sounds from libraries such as Big Fish Audio and Sonomic.

FL Studio is the Windows-only sequencer formerly known as Fruity Loops (www.fruityloops.com); Girl (www.girl.yowstar.com) is another new Mac-only loop based jamming tool with a scary interface; radiaL (www.cycling74.com) is a new loop-based jamming/performance/experimentation tool with an interesting interface, and MIDI control, effects plug-ins, and real-time record to disc, which lacks Live's ability to move seamlessly between 'composition' and 'performance', but makes up for it with its experimentation and interesting sound design applications;

Numerology (www.five12.com) is a Mac-only modular sequencer with AU hosting, rooted in the principles of old-school hardware step sequencing; and Pro Tools Free (www.digidesign.com) is what it says – a stripped down – but still very worthwhile – free version of Pro Tools for Mac OS (not OSX yet) and Windows.

Plug-ins and VSTi's

VST, VSTi, AU, TDM – whether you're using a performance tool like Ableton Live or a more studio-bound sequencer like Tracktion, plug-ins are an important addition to your sound. Plug-ins can take the form of effects, or software 'instruments' like synthesisers or samplers. Judicious use of these fun little add-ons can bring a new dimension to your sound. But don't overdo it!

Quote

They're designed to mangle sound in hopefully almost impossible ways – that's what makes a good plug-in for me! IriXx

MDA Autopan plug-in as seen by Tracktion.

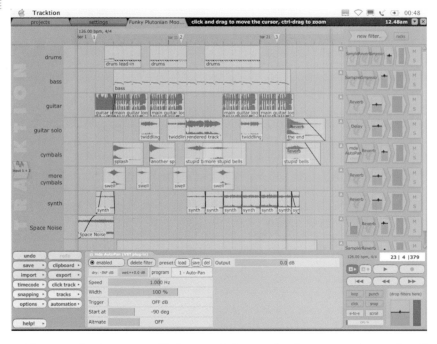

There are few laptop-specific issues relating to plug-ins, except the usual stuff about how the reduced capabilities of a laptop versus a desktop will give you slightly less headroom if you try to run too many plug-ins at once!

Just as plug-ins come in different formats, they come in different price brackets – free, expensive, and everything in between. Most high-end plug-ins tend to relate to production and mixing; studio tools, in other words. Further down the price scale, you find the more eccentric or just crazy sounding plug-ins, as well as some more conservative types that are still useful for performance or production. You might find that you never need to spend money on plug-ins; there are so many free ones around (though I'm sure the developers would appreciate a donation).

You can start by going to www.mda-vst.com and grabbing all the free stuff you can carry. Paul Kellett has created MDA VSTi synths and VST effects for Mac OS9/OSX and Windows, including Piano, ePiano, Combo (amp and speaker simulator), Dynamics (compressor/limiter/gate), Overdrive, RezFilter (resonant filter), Round Panner (3D panner), and Sub-Bass Synthesizer.

After that go visit Destroy FX at www.smartelectronix.com, where you will find top-quality free AUs and VSTs by Marc and Tom7, including geometer, scrubby (very cool), transverb, rezsynth, and skidder. Some of the DFX stuff is pretty hard to describe, it's better if you hear it for yourself! (Don't forget that donation!)

• *Yamaha have something very like scrubby on their SU700 and 'A' series samplers. That's one of the reasons I liked scrubby; I thought after I got rid of my SU700 I'd never be able to make that sound again, then scrubby came along. Ableton Live comes with some very very good plug-ins with good quality presets, but you can use VST plug-ins or probably soon AUs as well.* mindlobster

Move on to Green Oak's website at www.greenoak.com, for Mac VSTs by Glenn Olander – Phaserifier, Chorusifier, Delayfier, Spectrafier (verrrry useful), Excitifier,

Tracktion and DFX's scrubby.

and Tunifier. This is also the home of the excellent Mac/Windows AU/VSTi synth Crystal, a semi-modular software synth featuring both subtractive synthesis and frequency modulation, built-in effects, wave sequencing, granular synthesis, program morphing (this alone is a reason to get Crystal), and sound font support. There is a good stream of updates, and extra patches and banks are available. Crystal is a fine sounding synth for any money, but of course it's free! I particularly enjoy the patch breeding feature, where a new patch can be created from two others, a 'father' and a 'mother', with a controllable amount of random variation – this feature alone is a great source of material.

That's just some of the free plug-ins out there; it seems likely that more will become cross-platform as it becomes easier for developers to produce plug-ins for XP, OSX, and Linux.

Once you start paying for plug-ins, it gets really crazy – it's a full-time job to keep up with the new arrivals and updates. I just pulled out a sampler, a synth, and an effects package as examples:

Steinberg's (www.steinberg.com) HALion VSTi sampler – supports numerous formats including AIF/WAV/Akai/EMU/Giga/REX/Roland; huge amount of supplied content; up to 16 channels, 12 virtual outputs, a lot of disk space and a lot of RAM

Halion.

essential. Although it's usually associated with Cubase, I successfully used HALion with Tracktion.

D'Cota (again from Steinberg) is a VSTi synth, which I used with Tracktion and Metro. My personal use of soft synths rarely strays beyond the preset scheme of things – I prefer to do my sound tweaking on samples, or else I will record a synth part to disk using a preset, then edit it a lot afterwards using plug-ins in something like Ableton Live. D'Cota uses three different types of synthesis: advanced analog, spectrum, and wave impulse – I don't know what these mean; I found D'Cota a little discouraging, because it has relatively few preset sounds – I would say the emphasis is firmly on experimentation and creating your own sounds, so if that's your thing, you should look at it. I also tried D'Cota with a Mac OSX utility called HostX (http://mmturner.home.mindspring.com), which lets you open VSTi's in standalone mode – this can be useful for jamming in a simple environment, rather than having to deal with an on-screen sequencer. Full editing of the VSTi parameters are still available, and so is input from a MIDI source such as a keyboard; the audio output can also be recorded to disk.

Metro and D'Cota.

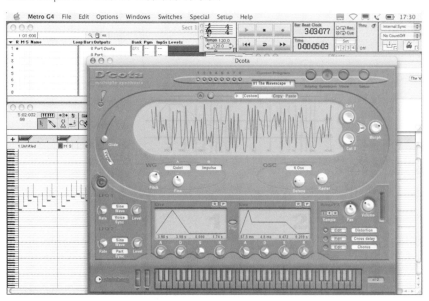

Cycling 74's Pluggo (www.cycling74.com) is a classic set of over a hundred plug-ins and synth instruments from the people who brought Max/MSP into the world, with VST, RTAS, and MAS compatibility. Effects include delay, filters, distortion, pitch effects, and synth instruments, but Pluggo excels in providing sounds that you're not likely to ever find in a 'professional' package. Max/MSP users can create their own Pluggo plug-ins, as well as plug-ins which can be distributed for use by non-Pluggo users.

Plug-ins – whether effects or instruments – are equally useful in the studio and in performance. There are people in the laptop world whose performances more or less constitute playing the plug-ins rather than working in a song-based linear way. The only problem with plug-ins is that when a new one comes along, it quickly does the rounds, it gets cracked – you hear it everywhere for a while, then suddenly it's old news, and it gets dropped in favour of the latest model. It's always fun to get new stuff to play with, but to blindly follow the 'new is best' path is a mistake; indeed, some laptop jammers I know are de-emphasising their use of plug-ins, and removing them from their drives, keeping only the very best ones, and instead relying on other factors to create a distinctive sound – like their choice of sample material, and their ability to program a good bass part!

I was made for plug-in you

These are all interesting plug-ins: maybe not the ones that everybody would choose, but your selection and implementation of plug-ins *should* be idiosyncratic – it's one of the ways to avoid sounding like everybody else! Crunch (www.monyetas.com/creed), Endorphin (www.digitalfishphones.com), XFade Looper (www.collective.co.uk/expertsleepers), Kantos (www.antarestech.com), Delay Llama (www.audionerdz.com), PSP Vintage Warmer (www.pspaudioware.com), THD (www.digitalfishphones.com), Zoyd (www.kvr-vst.com), Fish Fillets (www.digitalfishphones.com), Akai VZ8 sampler (www.akaipro.com).

Synths

I've already mentioned synths in passing – Crystal and D'Cota are both VSTi synths that need a host program to run within. There are other synths which run in standalone mode, or, more commonly, in standalone *or* plug-in modes. Native Instruments' Absynth (www.nativeinstruments.com) is one of the latter, formerly a Mac-only synth which has become cross-platform.

Absynth

In keeping with these new fangled modern times, Absynth uses more than several types of synthesis: granular, subtractive, wavetable, FM, AM, etc, as well as sampling. Absynth runs standalone, with a MIDI keyboard attached, or in plug-in mode as a VSTi/DXI/AU. Absynth comes with 800 presets, and it's obvious pretty quickly that it isn't a meat'n'potatoes sound module; the sounds are 'edgy', and broadly oriented towards techno/trance use (perhaps reflected in its ugly interface).

Rant

Before I go any further, I want to take a minute to beef about the various registration and copy protection schemes practised by software companies – can't we just agree on one system? And preferably one that doesn't require an internet connection for registration? Sometimes applications crash and need to be re-registered – not easy if it happens during a gig. It's all right for studio users, but for laptop users, who are just as likely for that crash to happen when they're roving around, it's just not viable.

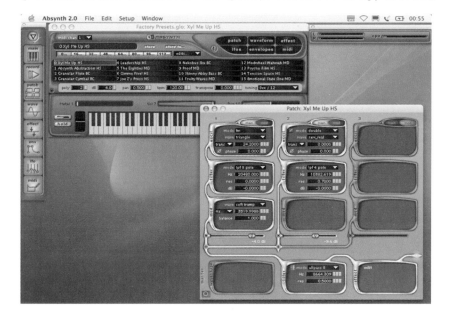

Absynth patch window.

Most of the presets are typical music shop demo fodder, with too many effects! The presets serve as an illustration of what's possible with Absynth, but they shouldn't be regarded as a library of ready to use sounds; you will need to do some tweaking of your own.

I reckon you should choose one synth which is closest to what you want, then work with it, get to know it. This might be better than knowing a little bit about a *lot* of soft synths; that's just not my way – I like the simplicity of a minimal set-up.

Unity Session

Bitheadz's Unity Session (www.bitheadz.com) could be described as a combination of their previous Retro AS-1 soft synth, and DS-1 sampler (both still available separately). Bitheadz seem to have a tough time of it; they don't get the recognition they deserve. Their software sounds great, but it does tend to have stability problems; I can only speculate that maybe Bitheadz aren't able to put adequate resources into it.

Unity Session Keyboard window.

In some ways, Session is laptop-*un*friendly, because it makes great demands on CPU and RAM, issues which are better dealt with on desktop computers. Session can function as a plug-in alongside Logic or Cubase or Digital Performer, et al, but it most frequently sees laptop action in standalone mode, with a keyboard attached. If you're a keyboard player who wants to go over to laptop use for porta-

Unity Session Editor window.

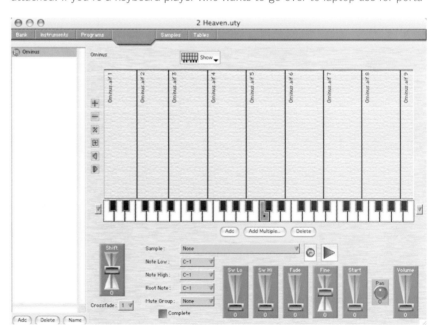

bility and flexibility of sounds, then that's where Session comes in, with a huge bank of preset sounds, and limitless sound design potential – you can work on your set at home or in the hotel with the same rig you use on stage.

I run Session in Mac OSX. It's far more stable than previous versions, and combining Retro and Unity into one package seems such a great idea I wish they'd done it sooner!

Like any good sampler/synth these days, Session is bundled with a lot of content – in this case, three CDs: Pop Drums Loops and Kits, Orchestral Strings Solo And Ensemble Strings, and Black And Whites Pianos – about 2GB worth of material. As well as using Bitheadz's own format, other sampler/audio formats are supported, including AIF, WAV, Gigasampler, SDII, sound fonts, Wave, MP3, Akai and Roland. Audio can of course also be recorded directly into Session and processed with a selection of effects. If your computer can handle it, Session can deliver 16 simultaneous channels, up to 24bit/96KHz quality, and 256 stereo note polyphony – but unless your computer is VERY state of the art, don't get your hopes up!

There are four different parts to Session, each dealing with a different aspect of the core application. Keyboard, which I already mentioned – a fast way of previewing/accessing sounds; Editor, where sounds are created or edited (presets can be tweaked and saved as new files), Player, with support for splits and layers, for use when playing with an external keyboard; and Mixer, a sixteen channel software mixer whose settings can be saved for future recall.

One of the good things about Session is its speed of setup (that's if you want to use it standalone). Get a keyboard connected, select a sound from the pull-down menus, and you can be jamming away immediately, and recording your output direct to disk as a stereo file in real time, which is great for capturing your noodling, then you can open it up in an editor, or move it into Ableton Live. Session also has a 'keyboard' mode which runs a minimal interface, featuring a small virtual keyboard; in this mode it's possible to trigger notes from your qwerty keyboard, and record that straight to disk. I've used this to quickly jam out a bass part, then open it in Ableton Live and start slicing/looping – so I guess that's laptop-friendly! It's a way of working without MIDI sequencers at all, using Session and Live to work in a more collage-y way.

Session sounds great straight out of the Mac. I get a kick from it that just isn't there for me with most soft synths. You can either use it as a library of presets or as a deep and profound sound creation machine. I also appreciate Session's no-frills interface, it's almost like it's built into the Mac OSX. However, it does demand a lot from you and your computer. Something as complex as this needs a large and easy to navigate manual, and it just isn't there at the moment. Bitheadz seem to acknowledge this with their 'lite' version of Unity and Retro, which have fewer sounds and less editability. The other problem is that under Mac OSX, Session insists on running in the background whenever other music apps were launched, putting quite a drain on system resources, and necessitating the use of Activity Monitor to force quit Session. Ugly. By the time you read this Session should also be available for Windows XP, in identical form to the Mac OSX version.

There's a growing library of additional content for Session, including drum kits, guitars, pianos, synths, and orchestral. One of the most interesting ones is Synth Expander SE1, which not only adds 600 new sounds to Session, but adds six further types of synthesis.

Moog Modular V

If Absynth and Session are too 'modern' for you, then take a trip down memory lane with Arturia's Moog Modular V (www.arturia.com). Totally at odds with Arturia's self-contained 'beginners' Storm app mentioned earlier, Moog Modular V is a high-end emulation of the classic Moog synth, with packaging and an interface to match. And corresponding CPU drainage.

Arturia Moog Modular V full window.

Modular V runs standalone with an external keyboard, or as a VST/AU plug-in. This one is going to appeal to hardcore synth fans, and probably less to others who will be content with Moogish sounds commonly available in other synths. If you've got no interest in creating your own sounds, you can use the supplied presets, and they do sound great, but you'd probably feel like you were paying for something that you'd never make full use of. Because this is such a precise emulation of the Moog's interface, it has to be said that it's not exactly computer-friendly; mousing and clicking on those knobs is a bore. I suggest you hook up to an external keyboard with as many knobs and faders as possible, something along the lines of M-Audio's Radium or Edirol's PCR. It does sound great, and much better than many of those 'moogish' presets previously mentioned, however I'm not sure that it makes a lot of difference by the time it's buried in a finished mix.

Modular V would make a great educational tool, if you're interested in the history and techniques of synthesis. It's also a cheaper and more portable alternative to buying and transporting an original Moog, and it has the added benefits of staying in tune, having presets, and being MIDI controllable!

Spongefork

Yo-yoing abruptly back to the 21st century now, and again firmly in laptop territory. Spongefork (www.spongefork.com) is a laptop jamming app for Mac OS, that combines synthesis and sampling in a qwerty-friendly environment.

It's all Ryan Francesconi's fault:

- *The reason Spongefork was created was to attempt to instrumentize the laptop; at the time (1997) there was really no software in that category. Now there are some nice options, though still nothing as good as a real instrument made of wood! But I try...SF2 is also meant to be a usable studio tool as well.*

Spongefork is one of the top laptop jamming tools around (as long as you're a Mac user of course) – it's the one I most often turn to when I'm building new sounds, and I've jammed with it many times. The basic version is free, then there's a small payment for an upgrade which adds a couple of features, including the very important 'record to disk'.

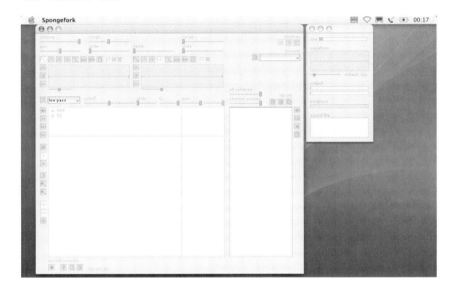

Spongefork – a great Mac OSX jamming instrument.

The main feature of Spongefork's mysteriously restrained looking interface is the XY area, where you click and drag to trigger sounds. These sounds can use Spongefork's synth-like qualities alone, or they can be a combination of synthesis and sampling – audio can be imported or recorded directly into Spongefork, and used either as sound mangling fodder, or as loops to play in the background while you're jamming. Up to twelve sounds can be looping simultaneously. Spongefork also records your performance/jam to disk, for use in another app – for example an editor or Ableton Live – or it could be reimported back into Spongefork. It's easy to get started with Spongefork, just click and drag, and try out the presets, though I recommend you watch your volume levels – it generates some pretty shrill tones! The presets can also be edited and saved (as can 'playlists' of imported loops), to create your own library of sounds.

Given Ryan's intention to create a performance instrument, it's natural that most of Spongefork's features can be accessed using keyboard shortcuts, which is helpful for live use, and there are rollovers which remind you of the necessary keys to push.

The 'instrument' intent is also evident in Spongefork's unwillingness to integrate with other apps – it is a hardcore standalone instrument; no VST, no Rewire, no MIDI, no nothing. You have to either just run Spongefork at the same time as other apps, without any direct sync or integration, or use the 'record to disk' feature and pop the resulting AIF into your favourite sequencer or whatever. Spongefork is a simple app to begin playing with – dumb luck and experimentation will yield good results; throw in a bit of 'study', and it gets even better.

Jam with what you just jammed — recycle yourself

When you're jamming with Spongefork, record a chunk of what you're doing to disk, and immediately import it back into Spongefork to use as a backing loop or load into an oscillator.

MidiFork

If even the user-friendliness of Spongefork is too much for you, you can have a ball playing with MidiFork (also from www.spongefork.com), a freeware X-Y interface which controls the MacOS's built-in QuickTime Instruments MIDI sound set. An instrument sound is assigned to each axis, and the tones can be constricted to chromatic or microtonal scales. Add pan and volume controls for each axis, and a big 'kill' button, and that's it! It can get pretty rackety, but since when has that been a problem?

Other apps

This is where the neither-fish-nor-fowl apps reside; software that requires new pigeonholes to be custom-built...

Melodyne

Celemony's Melodyne (www.celemony.com) is a piece of software that allows you to treat audio files like MIDI files. Sounds a bit like Ableton Live so far, doesn't it? But not so. Where Live is oriented towards loops and beats, and most of its time/pitch tools are focused on rhythmic alterations, Melodyne concentrates on melodic recordings, particularly vocals and solo instruments – individual notes in a recorded performance can be independently stretched, pitch shifted, and rearranged to an advanced degree. This can be done with the intent of 'fixing' a performance, or creating sounds or 'performances' that aren't possible in the real world. Add to that multitrack recording and VST/AU processing, and Melodyne becomes a pretty powerful sound creation tool.

Melodyne begins by analysing the pitch and tempo of the parts that you record or import into it (Melodyne will record multiple tracks simultaneously if you have an appropriate interface) – as Celemony say, it 'understands' the nature of the recorded/imported material, and applies what it considers appropriate algorithms. Following that, every aspect of the recording can be edited – as you make changes, Melodyne uses its previous analysis of the audio to preserve the character of the material, but sometimes the fun happens when you deviate from 'reality'.

There are two versions of Melodyne – Studio and Cre8. The major differences between them are that Cre8 supports a maximum of eight tracks at resolutions of up to 48KHz/24bit, and will only playback stereo files, while Studio has an unlimited track count (or as many as your computer can deal with), resolutions up to 192KHz/32bit, and will also allow the editing of stereo files. There is quite a price difference between the two, and for laptop use, where processor power is usually

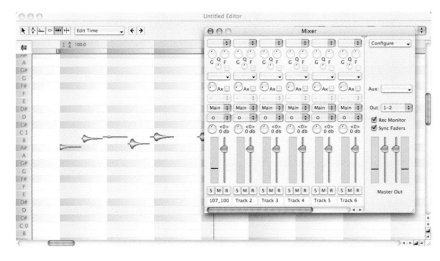

Melodyne – complex and creative.

in shorter supply, it might not be necessary to pay the extra for the Studio version.

Originally released as a purely standalone product, Melodyne is now more sociable when it comes to other software – it comes with Melodyne Bridge, a feature that allows Melodyne to behave as if it were a plug-in within a sequencer. Melodyne also features Rewire support, and this is the means of inter-app communication I usually use with Melodyne.

Melodyne has two main work areas – the Define Melody window, which displays audio waveforms for each track in your project, and the Edit window – where individual tracks are manipulated, and the fun stuff happens. If you're familiar with traditional MIDI sequencing, then you won't have any trouble relating to Melodyne – it just replaces audio files for MIDI files (kind of). It will also work as an audio-to-MIDI converter – once you've loaded, analysed, and edited your performance, the resulting notes and any other information such as pitch bend and volume, can be exported as a MIDI file, or just sent in real-time to your software synth of choice. This is a cool effect, and an interesting way of generating new synth parts from vocals, instrument parts, or speech. Melodyne also has a basic software mixer, with the typical mixer fixtures and fittings – pan, volume, solo, mute, and the ability to add third-party plug-ins, though I found I preferred to use Rewire and add other effects and controls in Live.

Melodyne works better with some source material than others. It works great with vocals and solo instruments, but it doesn't like chords or ensemble performances. It also helps if the recordings are as clean as possible; effects such as reverb in particular should be a voided. It can also be used to manipulate drum parts, though there's already plenty of apps that will slice/stretch/pitch drum loops.

Many of Melodyne's features can be assigned to control via external MIDI hardware, whether it's the typical mixer functions, or more Melodyne-specific actions. A MIDI keyboard can be used to playback the edited notes, or to edit the melody in real time.

You should quickly be able to tell if Melodyne is for you – it's a great example of an app which couldn't have existed just a few years ago. Initially I found some of its functions quite obscure, which may be more do with the interface than anything – the relationship between the two main windows isn't as clear as it might be, but there are helpful 'how to's on Celemony's website, and the manual has a few walkthroughs that help newbies like me get to grips with it a bit faster.

I can imagine creating tracks using just Melodyne and Ableton Live, nothing else; it has a lot of potential for people who aren't tied to working in traditional ways. Although initially there might seem to be some unnecessary duplication, their audio bashing assets actually complement each other superbly. Pitch and time are no longer related – in fact they're not even on speaking terms!

Using Melodyne

One way that Melodyne could be useful – if I get an idea for a vocal part, I will sometimes just sing it unaccompanied into a minidisc recorder or of course into my laptop's built-in mic. Later on, when I want to develop this vocal into a piece of music, I run into the old demo-itis...when I try to make a 'proper' recording of the part, it just doesn't sound the same, the spontaneity isn't there. Even though the original recording's quality leaves something to be desired, I want to use it. Because I recorded it a capella, though, it's not in time or in tune with anything in particular, which makes it difficult to add any pitched instrument parts. This is where Melodyne comes in! I can do some basic fixing, pushing the sung part to conform to recognisable pitches, and then if it's suitable for the piece, go into some experimentation too – choosing whether to keep it 'natural' or 'un-'!

Vokator

Native Instruments' Vokator (www.nativeinstruments.com) is a strange one – it's a vocoder for Mac OSX and PC, I knew that much before I started, and you probably knew that too. What I didn't know was that it takes the basic vocoding concept (applying the characteristics of one sound, typically a voice, to another sound, typically a synth. It's been used by (among others) Air, Daft Punk, ELO, Kraftwerk, and Stevie Wonder) and adds arpeggiators, sequencers, loop playback, sampling, effects, and synthesis, all of which gives it potential way beyond that of the traditional one-trick vocoder. Vokator has a lot of scope as a sound production tool...

With Vokator your sounds for input A can be a live input or a file on your hard drive, and input B can be live input or a wave or oscillator synth. Vokator is very CPU hungry, but if your laptop is able, then you could use it as a sophisticated live processor with MIDI parameter control. With the right computer (I must keep stressing that because Vokator will show your computer no mercy), and the right kind of live input, and a MIDI keyboard, it would be a great jamming tool, and I must say I find Vokator more interesting and creative than NI's other synth-based apps – even the interface didn't irk me as much as NI's usual efforts...still could be better though!

Vokator includes over 300MB of sounds to get you going, and many presets, and they make for good demonstrations of what's possible. It's pretty fast to get some live audio through, but watch out for feedback and sharp frequencies...protect your ears and your gear.

I was interested in Vokator even before loading it – I find the idea of something like Vokator much more exciting than 'JAFS' – Just Another F++++++ Synth'. These days mangling and distorting and processing and changing sounds collected from the real world – sampling! – is much more interesting than plain old synthesis. Of course, put 'em both together, and look out! Vokator goes some way towards addressing this; with a built-in synth, essential for a carrier wave anyway for the live input. If you were so inclined, Vokator could produce all your sounds, and Live could be the app for compiling them afterwards. Vokator works very well standalone, but can also be used as a plug-in within a host sequencer (where it will

Vokator – a vocoder for Mac and PC, and a whole lot more!.

appear as an effect and an instrument), which is useful for automation, MIDI control, saving/recalling settings, and so on.

Although it's very demanding in terms of CPU, and the interface has too many 'knobs', Vokator qualifies for inclusion on the strength of its standalone potential for real-time work with live inputs, and for its plug-in integration with Live. If like me, you prefer to use real-world sounds as your starting points for manipulation and jamming/composition, then you must try Vokator.

Midikeys

Sometimes the things that improve your musical life and workflow aren't the sexy applications or the status-boosting hardware, but the little extras and utilities that you call on every day. MidiKeys by Chris Reed (www.monyetas.com/creed) is just

MidiKeys - qwerty-to-MIDI utility; very useful for laptop music.

like that. It's a freeware Mac OSX app which will let you send MIDI notes from your qwerty keyboard to any MIDI application on your computer. Because it uses Apple's CoreMIDI technology, it should work with anything. This is a beautifully simple laptop-friendly thing – it means you can input notes in 'real time' without having to connect a MIDI keyboard. It's very handy – if I could use it to send program changes and channel changes via qwerty as well then I'd probably use it on stage and leave my keyboard at home!

Alphabet Soup

There are a couple more qwerty-based apps around, and I think it will be (or *should* be) a growing thing, driven by demand from laptop musicians. Eventually there will be one killer qwerty-based laptop jamming app; it's just a matter of time. Alphabet Soup (www.ozmusiccode.com) is a recent arrival, and sits somewhere between Midikeys and Live. It's a very minimal (but cute) looking app, which puts a representation of the qwerty keyboard on your screen; sound files can be drag'n'-dropped to each key – these can be loops, one-shot clips or entire songs, and audio formats can be mixed freely – wav, aif, snd, or mp3, with resolutions of 8, 16 or 32 bit. Separate volume and pan settings are available for each key; it's also possible to have multiple 'keyboards' open at once. This is a simple and fun-looking application which for some people will be just what the doctor ordered; it's a very immediate way to deliver a selection of clips or songs, and I know that there are new features coming along which will make AS even more interesting as a performance instrument.

Alphabet Soup – loops or entire songs on qwerty keys.

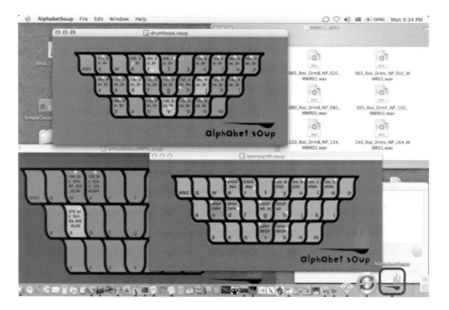

Junxion (www.steim.com) is one that fits right in here. I've already mentioned it in the 'hardware' section, but in brief it's a utility which allows any USB input device – mouse, joystick, game pad, graphics tablet – to send MIDI notes and control information. If you're looking for an individualistic solution to the thorny MIDI controller issue, then Junxion is your friend – invite it over to play at your place, but make sure you do your homework first.

Max/MSP

There is a certain type of laptop musician who scorns commercial software, who is only happy using apps which he has created himself. Most of these people are using Max/MSP (www.cycling74.com) to do their dirty work. Max/MSP is described by Cycling74 as a 'graphical programming environment', where various 'objects', each of which performs an individual task, can be visually linked together on screen

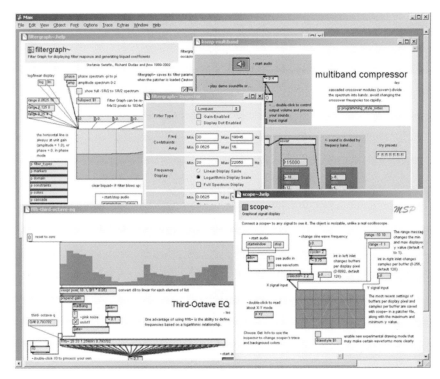

Max/MSP in Windows XP.

using virtual cables (to somewhat different effect than the system used by Reason, however). The 'Max' part includes the basic environment and MIDI functions; the 'MSP' part (there is also Jitter, which includes objects optimised for video and graphics) supplies the audio processing objects, including synthesis, sampling, signal processing, surround, simultaneous hard disk recording and playback, VST plug-in hosting, and support for many audio file formats. A completed Max project is called a patch.

After a long life as a Mac-only tool, Max/MSP has recently become available to Windows XP users too. It's a *highly* techy, and dare I say academic approach to music making, but it is very popular with laptop musicians – people who are frustrated by what they see as limitations inherent in 'regular' commercial software design. Because of its long history (15 years), the Max/MSP beginner can get a lot of support from other users, as well as from the Cycling74 website. I must confess that I'm not currently a user – I'm deterred by the tinkering involved. But there are things about it that interest me – creating my own plug-ins, perhaps, or maybe making my own qwerty-based MIDI application...but that's for the future. I can't honestly tell you more – Max/MSP is another one of those things that should be in a book of its own. If you want to write your own music software, this is a good place to start (but see also PD – www.pure-data.org, and jMax – http://freesoftware.ircam.fr. Both of these are free 'equivalents' to the not-free Max/MSP).

• *I create a lot of music using a system called the Musographic which I have been working on for a couple of years. This is not a custom written piece of software, but is instead the utilising of software not intended for making music, for musical purposes. In this case, it is web-design software, basically Flash and HTML, where different musical elements are placed into Flash animations with corresponding graphics and the length of each animation is determined either by the decay of the sound, or by chance, or by number-systems. Then multiple amounts of the animations are embedded into an HTML page and switched on. It's great, because as a composer you have very little control other than the choosing of the different sound-elements themselves – the relationships between the sounds are left to decide where to place themselves and are constantly progressing as the piece develops and the juxtapositions alter. In many ways it's a kind of self-composing, self-playing mechanical music created on a laptop with a graphic component on top of that which of course brings it into the realm of multimedia art – and also functions as some kind of minimalist digital orchestration, which is an idea I quite like!* Ergo Phizmiz

Strange as it may seem: Quicktime Pro

It seems perverse to skim over such complex and sexy apps such as Absynth and Vokator, only to loiter recklessly in the vicinity of something as cheap and commonplace as QuickTime Pro (www.apple.com), but that's what I'm going to do. To paraphrase the proverb, while you're staring at the overpriced and overpackaged-bug ridden vapourware in the online store, you might be missing an unrecognised treasure lurking on your hard drive.

QuickTime is at the heart of all of Apple's multimedia operations, and the QuickTime Player is the standalone front end (also available for Windows), which will play movies, and sound files. Whenever you open the QuickTime Player you see an ad which is trying to persuade you to upgrade to QuickTime Pro. I find this incredibly annoying, and usually I refuse to buy anything advertised this way. However, QuickTime Pro is worth the small price of an upgrade, and not just to make the ads go away.

It's possible to jam with QuickTime Pro and nothing else. I used to do it all the time, and, before Ableton Live appeared, I was planning to do some live shows using just QTPro. (When I said 'and nothing else', I lied. You also need an audio editor to capture and prepare your material – but why not use a free one like Audacity or Spark ME?!)

The trouble with QTPro is that it's quite shy. After paying your money you'll notice little difference in your QuickTime Player – except of course that the annoying ad has disappeared forever. And once you do make the effort to discover QTPro's hidden charms, the musical relevance of them might not be immediately apparent. The 'Pro' enhancements include: cut/copy/paste editing of audio and movie files with 'scale to fit' options, play movies full screen, loop backwards as well as forwards, create slide shows, create player 'skins' specific to your own project, and 'save as' and 'export' options for creating new versions of files and converting one file format to another.

QuickTime Player is available for Mac and Windows.

Here is an example of how QTPro can be used: I took a series of clips of a preacher speaking, recorded from a radio broadcast...some of the sentences I left complete, some as individual words, or even shorter – breaths, sounds, parts of words, the noises in between words. I saved each of these as a separate AIF file, then quit my editor and opened them all at once in QuickTime. I started them playing, one by one (make sure you uncheck 'play sound in frontmost player only' in QuickTime's preferences). I adjusted each one for maximum effect – panning a little left or right, adding or cutting bass and treble, choosing to loop forwards or sdrawkcab. I usually try to have between twenty and forty of these clips, filling the screen. If you play them all at once it can get ugly, but there are some nice effects that occur – it's impossible to get them all to start and end simultaneously, they are all different lengths after all, so just go with it. I find this kind of thing hypnotic, and I used these speech files on a couple of occasions, one being a jam with a Metallica style guitar player, and another with a laptop musician who was using Spongefork. If you've got an application that records all of your computer's audio, like Wiretap (www.ambrosiasw.com) or Audio Hijack (www.rogueamoeba.com), then you can capture these QT jams and use them as source material for future projects.

You can do a lot with a QuickTime Pro file. You can use the small black selection triangles to highlight areas on the timeline, and do simple cut copy and paste editing functions. You can use the equaliser and pan controls to modify the sound (slightly). You can loop entire sound files or parts of sound files – and you can also choose 'loop back and forth'. You can copy and paste several QuickTime files into one, and mix them down to a single stereo or mono file in various audio formats. As a step further from doing this, you can use the 'add scaled' command in the edit menu to scale the pasted clips to be the same length as the first 'target' clip. Of course this changes the pitch of the scaled clip, but who cares? This is a useful way of stretching one clip to match another. Once you've done the scaling operation you can use 'edit/delete tracks' to remove the reference clip and leave you with just the scaled clip. Make sure to choose 'save as self contained' when it comes to save your final file, so the new composite file isn't referring to any other files that might get moved/deleted later.

Important: all of this works with video as well!

This is appallingly low-tech, but that's how I like it. You don't have to spend a lot of money to have fun. It's a challenge to work against the limitations that these exercises impose on you. If you can't make something interesting using this, then you won't be able to do anything interesting using fancy 'high-end' stuff either!

- *I use standard stuff 'cos I'm not into tinkering. This may sound terribly naive, but I believe a product that's been r'n'd'd and has come out on a commercial release tends to be more stable and is easier to get support for than something that some guy's put together in his bedroom. You don't want that on stage. You don't want to be on stage just starting your gig and thinking 'some guy did this in his bedroom last night and I wonder what's going to happen now'!* mindlobster

Software piracy

Music software companies see thousands of copies of their products illegally made every year. This is usually described as 'music software companies lose ££millions', but it can't be proven that every act of piracy would otherwise be a purchase; personally I don't think so. But I do believe that you should pay for what you use. If you can't afford it, use cheaper or free software, and get a job. If you object to using commercial software because it's 'overpriced', or the copy protection measures somehow offend you, then don't use it, and don't be a hypocrite and use pirate copies either.

Though tempted I have been, it has always been easier to buy the software than to try to hunt down a cracked copy on the internet. JDG

(Do I use) Pirate software? No, but everyone I know does. I often question why I am struggling with the tools I can afford when there are so many who don't know how to use these awesome tools they downloaded. SongCarver

As a creator, I'm offended that people would even think about using cracks, and it grieves me to see how rampant piracy is in the music software biz. David Das

Sampling – in non-praise of the synthesizer

- *As far as soundscape music goes it's important not to use pre recorded CDs. It's part of finding your own sound – I think half the fun of what I do is the discovery process of finding sounds, finding things that I didn't expect. It leads me to look at the world in a different way. I have certain processes that I use; I walked past the Lloyds building one Sunday afternoon and it was dead quiet. I heard the air conditioning system making an interesting noise, so I started wandering around with my minidisc recorder.* IriXx

Being equipped with a computer that allows you to record and compose on location can have a profound effect on your music – you may find it more interesting to sample and manipulate environmental sounds than to work with sterile presets from a software synthesiser. Applications like Ableton Live have brought back the joys of old-school sampling – with a few modern knobs on. Sampling can be about more than getting drum loops or hits, or lifting a vocal from somewhere – creating loops from highly processed chunks of noise, then jamming with these, recording and remanipulating the results, and doing it again.

- *I am pretty adamant about only creating my own sounds, via old equipment and resampling my own works. Old keyboards are often the sources – mostly cheap nasty and broken, especially Casio ones!* Douglas Benford

You should start by recording your environment. Any sound can be fodder for your music, and don't discard things because they're too obvious – try it all!

- *One of the immediate benefits of using a laptop to make music is obviously portability. I compose using as many sounds as I can find – I'm often seen stood around large shrubs in Lincolnshire holding a laptop and pointing a little computer mic at the bees. There's a certain limitlessness to what you can record with a laptop – I love the idea that you can be anywhere and collect sounds. Obviously you can do this with a minidisk or a tape machine, but the benefit of using a laptop is that it compacts all this studio equipment into one area, and also permits on-the-road editing – so you can literally record and edit on the bus. Of course sound is everywhere, so you can literally find amazing source material anywhere – the pizza shop, your living room, every corner of the garden, you know, anywhere.*   Ergo Phizmiz

I'm not a synth-hater by any means – I use them all the time because I like to mix my 'environmental' sounds with more straightforward instrumentation. To me that's the best of both worlds – the sounds you record yourself will counter the sterility of the software-generated synth sounds.

- *I remember watching a guy doing field recording of birds on Walthamstow Marshes, which is a nature reserve, and he was wandering around with his laptop open like some 21st century water diviner saying 'please mug me I've got an expensive computer". I'd much rather shove a minidisc in my pocket, and a nice supply of cheap batteries and discs, then bring it back and archive it.*   J-Lab

Collecting sounds is easy, too – you don't need a lot of gear. If your laptop has a built-in mic, then use that (but exercise some discretion about where you pull it out). Failing that, minidisc recorders are good, especially if used in conjunction with an unobtrusive t-mic. Failing *that*, then it's whatever comes to hand – recording cassette machines, digital voice recorders, those keyrings that record 8 seconds at a time, whatever it has to be.

- *I do most of my field recording with a Nagra or a Tascam portable DAT machine. It's a bit more solid to work this way than to lug a general-purpose computer out into the field.*   Luke

What you record is up to you – sometimes it's a big loud obvious sound, sometimes it's like listening in close-up; getting some small, quiet, background noise that you wouldn't normally be aware of. So start at home, and work your way outwards from there.

- *I use a minidisc. I've recorded anything from noises in between conversations on phones to lift noises, to background noise from machines. I suppose a strictly non-musical basic approach makes me get inspired by objects and concepts and the sound they make.*   Emilia Telese

Once you've recorded your cat snoring and the peas defrosting, you need to work on the recordings a bit to make them usable. For some occasions, 'usable' means just take them as they are and drop 'em into a track. On other occasions, it can mean carefully extracting particular slices from the recordings, and using Ableton Live and some plug-ins to convert them into interesting rhythm loops or textures. There's no right or wrong with this, it's just what sounds good to you. In time you'll identify 'good' parts faster, and your recording technique will change as you learn what your computer is capable of doing to the material afterwards. Live is such a good app for this kind of stuff – there's nothing better out there.

- *I also score for multimedia, and pre-packaged sound libraries make it easy for me to get consistent results.*   JDG

Sometimes though, you want a sound that you just can't record or create yourself, and this is where sample libraries come in. Sample libraries are also used by composers and other pro-types working on a deadline, who don't have the time to go

Soundshuttle opened from within Ableton Live.

out and record the sounds themselves. Until recently, this was exclusively a CD-based activity – sample CDs would come in either audio format, or (more expensive) sampler formats such as Akai or Emu, and Reason's Refills. The growth of software samplers has also spawned mini-apps such as Osmosis and Reload (www.bitheadz.com and www.propellerheads.se), software which is designed to help you translate your archived Akai (etc) format samples into forms that your computer will recognise. Time + Space (www.timeandspace.com) are the kings of sample CD distribution – their catalogue should be the first place you look if that's what you need.

If you're a laptop user who's into wifi though, then there's another option to CDs – getting your samples online. The most interesting development in this field has been PowerFX's SoundShuttle (www.powerfx.com) – a VST plug-in that allows you to preview any of PowerFX's 40,000-plus sounds (also available on CD and DVD), and then use your credit card to buy the ones you like. I think SoundShuttle is a great idea – you only pay for the sounds you want, no filler, and in theory it's a go-anywhere service (as long as you can get online). In a way it's not meeting an existing need, it's actually creating an opportunity for new ways of working. The only problem I can see – it's the wifi use that interests me, the being able to download new samples from wherever I am, and maybe wifi isn't universal enough yet. In the meantime however, it's still a great resource for studio use – an available library of thousands of sounds, without having to fill your hard drive.

- *Your own environment is the best place to get sounds, your own voice and any instruments you can play and it gets progressively worse from then on. I think if you're a professional composer or sound designer than it's a fair case for using sound libraries, because you haven't got time and you need certain things, specific things, but I think if you're doing your own creative projects than you should restrict yourself in terms of using those commercially available things, because it's much harder to have your own identity. Drums I think are very difficult, that's the thing I most often use from libraries. Even when you programme things like that yourself, when you bring in something recorded by somebody else, it can add an extra dimension to it.* mindlobster

Public Loop – Ableton Live and laptops in the classroom

*P*ublic Loop is a travelling project that brings laptops running Ableton Live and Arkaos into classroom situations with people who don't usually get access to that kind of thing. We've done projects with kids, based at local arts centres, and with offenders in medium secure psychiatric units.

For our first project, which was with kids, we used the venue's own desktop Macs, and just got the kids cutting, pasting and titling with QuickTime Pro, and we added library music from an external source. The class was very successful, but the preparation was a nightmare – the computers weren't all set-up the same way, and it took a long time to get them functional. It was clear that we needed to bring our own equipment into the classroom, just to get the quality control.

For our next project we spent some lottery money on hardware. At the time we'd run into a lot of resistance about bringing computers into secure environments; there was a lot of concern about security, people using them to get on the internet, smuggling things within the computers themselves – which we felt to be mostly unfounded, and primarily based on a lack of knowledge of how secure computers can be. We ended up using hardware sampling workstations, and hardware video editing decks. Again the course was highly successful, with unprecedented high attendances, and creating interest in literacy, computer studies, music technology, and digital art amongst students who were previously unwilling to attend any classes at all. However, the sheer bulk of the equipment worked against us, and on the occasions when laptops were introduced to the class on a test basis, it was clear that a laptop running music and video software simultaneously enabled a far more fluid and intuitive working situation. Initially some students were intimidated by the computers because of their illiteracy, but once they saw what was possible with them, they were won over – it was very exciting for them.

After that course, we took a long break and evaluated the situation; we decided to move over to a strictly laptop based set-up. We're all Mac users, so there was never any doubt about which platform to use. We bought a few second-hand iBooks, and managed to get some very appreciated support from software companies, so we didn't have to pay for any software, which would have been difficult to manage at that point (and we didn't want to use pirated copies).

Since then, the classes have been transformed. Students are learning the ropes much faster, which is great, especially when you consider the mix of learning difficulties, illiteracy, and computer inexperience we run into. Each student can capture their own photos, video, and sound, and work with all elements on the same computer – it breaks down the barriers between the forms, there's no need to distinguish between them, and it's usually easy to lead the students into 'non-traditional' ways of working, along more experimental lines. Set-up is faster, and travelling is much easier – the classroom equipment can be moved on a bus or train instead of relying on a big car being available.

Grace Connor, Creative Director, Public Loop

When a student's finished a project, we use the Airport cards to wirelessly send the files to the 'teacher' iBook, which is then taken back to HQ for posting on the website (www.publicloop.com), archiving to HD, and burning to DVD or CDRom.

Without the laptops, we could still do our classes, but the issues of transportation, moving between forms (music and video), archiving, and posting online would all be much harder – it just wouldn't be the same.
(Grace Connor, Creative Director, Public Loop)

Awkward question

Is there a stereotype of a laptop musician?

- *If there is, I´m probably too old for it (41).* Thomas Neuhaus

- *It's become a stereotype – shaven-headed guys in t-shirts making bleeping noises!* IriXx

There is a stereotype. White, male, skinny/undernourished looking, shaved head, jeans, khaki or similarly dull toned t-shirts. Performing glitch or techno or ambient dub influenced music. It's true. But it doesn't have to be that way – stereotypes are made to be busted! You don't have to be a geek. You don't even have to be particularly interested in computers, the amount of time spent fiddling under the hood can be minimal. If you want to tinker, fine, but luckily these days that's more of an option than a requirement; you can just get your computer running and spend all your time creating.

- *There's always someone who turns up with Max MSP and spurts out a terrible noise over everybody else. I think the worry is that the general public would see us all as one big grey mass.* Pendle

- *There are many female laptop artists; Granny Ark and Robin Judge (www.robinjudge.com) both are using laptops for what they do.* Neil Wiernik

- *Is it for boys only? If the question is 'should it be?' then the answer is no, if the question is 'is it?' then the answer is almost always yes, but that's the same with all computer stuff, there's that twitchy slightly, guy, geeky thing – most geeks are male. And most keen musicians, especially the ones that talk about it a lot, tend to be male anyway, so it's the ultimate combination of male character traits. Composition is a male dominated field, technology is a male dominated field, and performance can be quite macho and a testosterone driven thing also.* mindlobster

- *If you want to know if laptop music is for boys only, ask Vicki Bennett of People Like Us.* Ergo Phizmiz

- *Do I fit the stereotype? No, I'm a little too fat.* JDG

- *Unfortunately there seems to be a stereotype – a nerd or whatever. I think it's a bit unfair – it's the visible public side of a computer musician. It's the first time a lot of electronic musicians have been able to do that; you do find a lot of bands that will use one massive set-up in a studio and have to condense it live. There are a lot of pasty faced geeks, but the whole idea of having a laptop is that you can go outside and get a suntan and still get the work done, which is another motivation for getting a laptop. When I was on tour in places like Italy I would feel inspired and wish I had a music set-up with me. You can't drag a studio around on tour with you, but you can take a laptop.* J-Lab

Jamming

I'm using the term 'jamming' to cover all types of live performance – solo/group/improvisation/structured performance. It's important stuff, because it's in live performance that the laptop music scene finds its strongest reasons to exist, but the chapter is not too big – that's because jamming info is spread throughout almost every other part of the book.

- *I use my laptop live on stage regularly to replace racks of sound modules. Desktop computers have more power, so they're more suited to being serious studio computers, but laptops have great portability. The kinds of soft synths available go far beyond what's ever been possible with rack-mount synths, so it's opened up new sonic worlds. Desktops can do the same things; they just don't travel as well.* David Das

This is also the place to let laptop jammers talk about what they do, how they do it, and what they would like to do, so a lot of space is given over to their words; wise, rash, or otherwise...

Jam gear

Using a laptop and the associated portable gear means you can take your studio on stage with you – this has the advantage of familiarity – you don't need to reinvent the wheel as far as setting up your gear goes, and I find it helps me feel at home and comfortable on stage – everything is where I expect it to be.

Along the same lines, if you can manage to get them to the venue, it's a good idea to bring your own stands. This continues the familiarity theme, and ensures that you will get everything setup on stage the way you want. This is partly influenced by my feeling that laptop musicians should stand during performances – I believe it works better for audience and performer. If you're going to sit, then chances are good that any venue will have something you can use – stools, chairs, tables, boxes, etc, but it's unlikely that they'll have something of standing height. The best stands to use are folding projector stands, which will give you a large flat surface to work with (but are not usually height adjustable), or, for a slicker appearance, something like Ultimate Support's Ultimate Apex (www.ultimatesupport.com) – a single column stand with two tiers, which breaks down small and is very easy to transport – but not cheap! This is the solution that musicians such as David Das and Tom Scott have opted for.

When performing with just a laptop, and no external keyboards or controllers, I've used a folding metal music stand – they can easily take the weight of a laptop.

Whatever kind of stand you use, make sure it's stable – it's not good if your laptop hits the stage halfway through the gig.

Make the most of your display

High resolution displays, which are good for studio use, allowing you to fit 'more' on screen, can be harder to read at a glance on stage – say if you look down at your MIDI controller and then back to your display it can take a moment to orient yourself – so experiment with switching to a lower resolution and see if your life is easier with the 'larger' view of things. I do this when running Ableton Live, and find it really useful – though I have unusually bad eyesight!

And that reminds me; time to re-state the obvious – gigs are very high-risk events for laptops. Be careful!

Fortunately my laptop has not yet crashed during a performance, but has many times before a performance, causing much panic! I switched it off and on again and tried talking nicely to it and then it worked.

- *Somewhere on your computer have the registration numbers for all your software in case it decides to unregister itself halfway through your gig which can be inconvenient. Have a duplicate copy of your whole set on your drive, so if the original gets damaged you have a safety copy. Pre-render any greedy effects to save CPU, and don't use too many things like reverb because it can get very muddy through a bad PA.* mindlobster

- *Not crashing exactly, but I quickly had to move to another track to deal with the uncomfortable and sudden silence. Always have a backup.* Douglas Benford

Sometimes you can bring your friend Shade with you.

Jam world

The whole point of laptops is their portability, so if you're looking for a place to jam with your friends, you can be adventurous – and you can bet that anywhere you can think of to play, somebody's done it. Laptop jams have taken place in homes, cars, cafes, clubs, aircraft, on boats – everywhere that a laptop can go. Towards the end of summer 2003 the Brighton laptop jammers held a very successful evening event on Brighton beach. Brighton has a healthy and expanding wifi culture, which makes it a good host for laptop-based events; it's quite a strange experience to sit on Brighton beach with a laptop, and check your email, then open Reason and work on some drum parts – just keep the ice cream off your keyboard.

There is a problem with working outdoors, however – ten seconds after you lift the lid of your laptop, you'll discover what it is. The screens are useless in sunlight – despite the many ads that show happy businessmen and students working away in sunny exteriors. Shade is your friend.

Sometimes laptops are described as 'portable offices' or 'portable studios'; well, your portable office/studio/playpen can have walls too – buy a pop-up tent and get out there. Who wants to be sitting indoors on a nice sunny day, while the folkies are in the park frightening the birds with their acoustic guitars?

The moment of tent inspiration came while enjoying a cappuccino at the local park cafe, with my friend Miriam, another laptop jammer. We observed a family playing on the grass, the kid had a neat looking pop-up tent. We went over and had a look and a word about the tent – 'hey, that would be great for laptops!'. Within 24 hours we had been to several shops, tested a few models for size, and finally bought a pair of tents (I subsequently bought a third). They are great. They live in their own special bags, flat packed, and pop up in seconds. They keep sun off you, (light) rain off you, and they afford some privacy if you need it – it's a nice cocoon-like environment.

I spent a lot of the summer in various parks and on assorted beaches, writing, sleeping, and jamming in my tent, but it's more fun when there's two or more of you, a mini tent village, a mini festival. The tents are fun to be in, they are colourful and although shady, enough light gets through for you to see what you're doing. They have flaps so you can really shut the world out when you want to, with mesh windows and a large side opening to accommodate the linking tunnels which are also available. You really should try this – I'm six feet tall, and can fit in the tent comfortably, with enough room to curl up and go to sleep when the mood takes me. See you on the beach. Or in the park.

Jam behaviour

- *I have jammed with other laptop users in the past; there were three of us going at once at one time. Oh yeah, and I have jammed with somebody playing guitar, Barry playing Metallica guitar, and me on laptop, that was cool because he was totally unused to that kind of thing, and he dealt with it quite well. I would really like to try jamming with a percussionist.* mindlobster

- *I come from a jazz/new music background. I'm improvising live with different lengths of digital audio snippets that I can mix, trigger from a sequencer or play through the LADSPA plug-in library. I've played with acoustic and electric players, but I still see my core act as being solo improvisation. I studied flamenco with Miroslav Tadic and Jazz with James Newton and Les Coulter, so I have a big acoustic guitar background.* Brian Redfern

If you jam a lot with the same people or person, and you don't want to get stale, try to impose some arbitrary rules to work against – limitations can provoke you to discover new things. These are some of the 'rules' that I've used in jams with other people – and I should add, record *all* of your jams!

1 Time limits – start with 30 seconds, then work your way upwards.
2 Swap samples – it's quite 'interesting' to be thrust into a jam with somebody else's sounds!
3 Only one sample each for the jam – pushes you into exploiting the material at hand.
4 Along similar lines – everybody jams with the same sample!
5 Dry – no plug-ins allowed!
6 Introduce other instruments – guitars, vocals, percussion, accordion, etc.
7 Allocate different parts of the stereo spectrum to each jammer, ie left/right if

there's two of you.

8 Allocate different frequency ranges to each jammer.

9 Allocate different 'voices' to each jammer, ie one does beats, one does speech, one does bass.

10 Take turns running each other's output through one of your Live channels, and mangling their performance.

This marathon solid-gold contribution from SongCarver:

In the end, make sure your music has something to say. It's a terrible feeling at the end of the night when everybody's interested in your technology, but not in your songs or message. Makes you feel hollow. – I know the feeling :-(

- *Be pragmatic, not dogmatic. For example, in Live you cannot open multiple songs, so just have QuickTime play a segue between tracks.*
- *Don't rely on any one piece of equipment.*
- *If it isn't reliable throw it away.*
- *I have a foldable ironing table – it makes for an excellent keyboard/laptop/mixer stand. Just gaffer tape everything on to it and you can move on and off stage very quickly.*
- *If you use it in the studio you will want to use it on stage.*
- *(USB bus powered) Controller keyboards are MAGIC for performing. No MIDI leads, no power leads.*
- *Wall warts will break. Avoid.*
- *Don't be afraid to do part of your stage show with NO technology at all. It's a performance, not a tech showcase.*
- *Practice playing laptop stuff standing up – it's very different and weird.*
- *Do anything to get away from that screen! Please! Or at least project it for the audience.*
- *Don't accept the norm. Whether that be software, hardware anything. I think the accordion interface could be an amazing way to interface with a computer; it has all the right characteristics.*

And the problem with software is that it is so visual. I don't know about you but I find that it is a huge leap from 'being' on stage and 'looking at a computer' on stage. By that I mean it is a mental gear-change for the performer; a difficult and stupid gear change in my opinion. I would rather be looking at the audience, looking at fellow performers, reading a score, or looking into space and listening.

Experiment with more hardware controllers – make your own. The commercial ones are stuck in the 1950's. I would like to see a trend to having the laptop person sitting side-on to the audience, in the way that a classical pianist sits.

SongCarver's glove interface

Before I tell my story, I'll issue the standard warnings: I am not liable for any damage you do to yourself or any equipment if you try to duplicate this idea. If you wire something wrongly you may damage your computer beyond repair!

Building my glove interface extended over about four months, lots of Googling, and a few trips to my local electronics store. It didn't cost a lot of money, and it now allows me to do quite a lot in general. It always grabs attention at gigs and I'm asked every time about it afterwards.

So, what is it, and why did I build it? One of my recent performance projects was called 'The Knice project'. It was a little play on words which melded 'easy listening/ambient' (nice) music with the cutting edge in technology (knife). Basically I would play acoustic guitar, run that through my PowerBook via Ableton Live and output a mix of acoustic sound and DSP effects/ loops.

Using the software and guitar at the same time was tough. I had thought about MIDI foot pedals to control the software, but finding things with my feet seemed to draw ability away from my fingers; and I'm no great guitarist. Extra switches on my guitar did not provide a perfect solution either, for similar reasons.

Then came the idea of a glove which would allow me to make some sort of 'sign language' to control the computer. The glove idea piggybacked on the human body's kinesthesis* allowing control without looking at it. (*Kinesthesis is the mechanism which provides calibration feedback from your muscles, allowing you to position them accurately with no visual feedback. You can prove this by closing your eyes, spreading your arms out, then slowly bringing your two index fingers together until they touch. Cool eh?)

Now, don't get me wrong. I knew that glove controllers were an old idea. In fact, many current high-quality MIDI glove designs exist, mostly in universities. They usually provide many streams of continuous data – finger extension, hand position in 3D space, etc; many systems can understand 'gestures'. And quite a few years ago there was the Nintendo Powerglove which provided many of these features in a cheap, commercially produced toy. My aspirations were not so high – I simply wanted ways to trigger recording, turn effects on and off, and play back pre-recorded loops.

I considered the commercial sensor-to-MIDI interfaces, like the i-cube (www.infusionsystems.com), but they were out of my price range. I looked at the options of building a customised MIDI device, using programmable chips (www.ucapps.de). That solution did not seem right for me – I didn't want to do *that* much soldering!

So, I looked at how other people were finding ways to interface with a computer in a simple way. One website explained how to build arcade machines at home. You know, so you can put in a dollar and play a game of Double Dragon in your lounge room. In these designs, a normal PC keyboard was hacked to use external buttons to generate keystrokes. Although the hack would not produce MIDI data, Live is easily controlled by keystrokes, and it's easy to set up.

The site explained how most USB PC/Mac keyboards run on a 'grid' idea where contact 'A' touches contact '5' to generate keystroke 'G''. I equated this to 'thumb touches index finger to generate G'. Having bought a cheap generic PC keyboard, I removed the circuit and did some testing – it worked. I now needed the interface itself; I'd read about glove interfaces using lycra with intricate metal thread contacts. I needed something more, well, feasible.

The solution turned out to be a thin leather glove (ladies, I think!), bought second-hand for $2. It was durable, fitted well, allowed me to cut out the fingertips with minimal fraying, and allowed any sweat to pass through. For contacts I eventually arrived at the solution of cutting up an aluminium cola can, sanding off the lacquer, and cutting shapes from it to attach to the glove. After some fiddling, I found the right shapes and positions for the contacts so that they would not accidentally trigger when I played guitar. I used gaffer tape to secure the aluminium. (hot glue gun in

SongCarver is an Australian musician/performer who has developed an unusual way to interface with his computer – a glove.

future). For cabling the glove to the circuit I used some parallel port cable with socket – it's nice to be able to disconnect and just walk away (Ethernet cable in future).

During this stage, I was working in a call centre to pay the bills. Hundreds of times a day I would be sitting in front of a PC, headset on, idle for a few minutes. So I decided to use that time to strip the wires and trim sections of the aluminium. Sitting at my computer, cutting up wires and assembling circuitry used to give the networking IT guys nightmares!

The end result surprised even me for reliability and usability – with one extra feature: holding down any finger and thumb combo triggers the 'autorepeat' function of the keyboard – a cool 'stutter' effect, quantised in Live into 1/16th notes. The little circuit board from the PC keyboard I kept in a tiny tupperware container, and decided to add one more feature – a super-bright blue LED to the top of my glove – a torch for a dark stage.

Since building my glove I have found a great little piece of Mac software called JunXion (http://www.steim.org/steim/junxion.html), which converts data from joysticks and other USB controllers into MIDI data. (There are similar programs for Windows.) This allows any USB controller to become a MIDI controller. My next step is to utilise this program with a hacked joystick to generate continuous controller (CC) messages from my glove.

One other factor you want to keep in mind is wireless. Trust me, having leads anchoring you is a bummer. There are now many wireless keyboards and joysticks around. One other nice factor about wireless is that you cannot blow up your computer if you wire the wireless keyboard or joystick wrongly. Just don't futz with the receiver bit connected to the computer.

Some other future implementations would be lights on the glove which flash when an action is performed. This sounds like silly theatre, but I found most audiences couldn't quite understand what I was doing with the glove. In fact, freedom from the laptop screen is one of the greatest benefits. Most laptop performers could be checking their e-mail for all the audience knows. My aim is take it even further – to be able to control the computer without looking at it at all. Much like you can play guitar chords without looking, or play trumpet with your eyes closed. Adding haptics (http://touchlab.mit.edu/). Make my glove 'tap' when a loop is triggered, and 'rumble' when CPU usage is getting too high – conversing with the computer with touch, pressure and force.

Hope this article proves useful – you can find me, my music and projects at www.songcarver.com.

The do's and don'ts of laptop gigs

2002 was my year of the laptop gig. I sold my hardware sequencer and sampler, and went Mac only. Now, many months later, as I take a break from gigging to work on a CD, it seems a good time to review – and to share the dubious benefits of my experience. Maybe you're already gigging yourself, or maybe you're just about to embark on the uniquely 21st century experience of standing in front of an audience while you tap away at a qwerty keyboard; whatever, there is something here, in no particular order, for all of you...

Do
- Close all apps that you don't need, and disable sleep/energy savers/screensavers.
- Have an on-screen checklist of pre-gig things to do.
- System volume maximum, alert sounds minimum.
- Bring your mains adaptor.

- Have some visual interest.
- Get gigs with non-laptop acts. You will stand out more.
- Perform standing up. It looks less like you're doing your homework, and creates a different vibe for the gig.
- Bring a mini jack stereo to 1/4' l-r lead – they haven't got one at the venue.
- Try playing actual music instead of just playing your plug-ins – the audience will thank you for it.
- Get a hard case for your laptop. This can also double as a riser if your stand/table isn't high enough.
- Use a MIDI-USB hardware controller to add some much needed spontaneity to your set.
- Ask the promoter if your laptop is covered on his/her insurance. Go on, ask them, just for a laugh.
- You are probably performing in a venue where beer and other alcoholic beverages are available. These do not mix well with laptops. Careful. And god forbid anybody throw anything towards the stage…
- Get backup. Make duplicate copies of your files, bring any app CDs/passwords you think you might need. Have a plan for what to do when your computer crashes. Sooner or later it will. Have a second laptop ready to go, or have a CD ready to play. I have a track ready on my iPod, in play/loop mode, with volume at zero, running throughout my set, so that if I need to I can unplug my iBook and connect the iPod, then bring the volume up, and then fix the iBook. Haven't needed it yet, but it's just a matter of time…

Don't

- Assume that the venue will have enough power points. Charge up before leaving home!
- Leave your laptop unattended. At all. Not for a second.
- Add any new hardware/interfaces/software (especially updates) within 2 weeks of a gig – computers hate surprises, and they will punish you.
- Forget the remote control for your video projector. You have got a video projector, haven't you?
- Be afraid to make mistakes. Your whole career is probably a mistake anyway!
- Get overexcited and abuse your precious laptop in an effort to look 'rock'n'roll'. If you're gigging with a laptop nobody's gonna believe it's rock'n'roll whatever you do!

Awkward question

Can you have a distinctive sound with a laptop?

- *I can, but no-one else can. It's a curse I think. But I am trying, and one day I will not have a unique sound.* Mochip

- *I've found that the limit to your sound is your own making. So yes, I'd say you can have a unique sound using one.* Lionel Valdellon

- *I just listened to the first piece of electronic music I made, it was made with CSound on an SGI in 95. it sounds very much like the music I still make today.*

The technology has really only allowed to me to work faster and more efficiently. JDG

- *An iBook or Sony Vaio does not have a trademark sound, but some software HAS.* Douglas Benford

Laptop jams in London and Brighton

I had heard about the laptop jams – founded by Arizonan Stuart Smith and German Lars Schuy, running regular events at the Hanbury Arms Ballroom in Brighton. And I had seen their website (www.laptop-jams.com), where it says 'sonically galvanised video pixeldelia'. I had never made it to one of their gigs, I just didn't get down to Brighton that often.

When I heard about their short season of events at the London ICA, it seemed the perfect time to drop in and see what was going on (as long as I didn't have to pay for a ticket of course).

Rather than using a dedicated room, the jam was taking place in the ICA's bar, with the 'performance' area crammed into a corner by the stairs, and a small PA delivering the 'performance' to the bar clientele. The audience consisted mainly of people who were there to see other events at the ICA, just killing time and getting a drink before their friends turned up, or before their movie started, so it was interesting to observe their reactions and non-reactions to the laptop generated entertainment. I suspect most people didn't even realise there was a jam in progress, so low-profile and non-showbiz were the proceedings. Somebody I talked to at the bar wasn't getting it – they said: 'I don't know if I'll come back; I like to dance – I can't dance to this.'

There were six 'workstations' available – three video laptops facing three music laptops. The video laptops were routed through a Panasonic video mixer to a video projector, and the music laptops were sent to the PA via a small mixer. A few people had brought along MIDI/USB controller devices, such as Evolution's UC16, but

most were simply using the qwerty keyboard. The laptop jam site has a few pertinent words about controllers:

> *No keyboards or keyboard playing! MIDI controller units are cool, as are the little Oxygen type units, but if you turn up with a 6 octave controller keyboard it'll be staying in the case. Richard Clayderman was bad enough the first time round.*

So I think it's clear where they stand on that one.

Everybody who jammed audio was using Ableton Live, whether on a PC or Mac (Ableton have subsequently become sponsors of the laptop jams) – Live has come to dominate the field, and there seems no sign of that changing; it's almost as if Ableton invented laptop performance! There was more diversity on the video jamming side – I was expecting to see Arkaos in use, but instead the video apps of choice were things like MotionDive (www.motiondive.com), Image/ine (www.image-ine.com), and VDMXX (www.vidvox.net).

The set was divided into two – a one-hour 'mellow' set, then a half hour break, then a one-hour 'manic' set. As usual with laptop music, and especially with such a deliberate non-image, it was hard to get any sense of 'performance' from the sets; there seemed to be a lot of recurring common elements – a consensus sound; a polite way of saying 'the lowest common denominator', perhaps. Maybe three people jamming like this is too many, unless there's an understanding about who will do what, so everybody isn't fighting for the same sonic turf.

Some of the music was great, some of it was rubbish, but if you've ever jammed with any kind of instruments before, then you'll know that's what happens!

Over subsequent sessions the format was revised – mindful of the obscurity of their actions, the jammers positioned themselves on a row of tables in the main bar area, facing the wall, so that bystanders could watch over their shoulders. This created a much better atmosphere, and a situation where the curious could simply wade in and start asking questions.

I approached laptop jams cautiously; I've had my fingers burned before with 'special interest groups', but they are open and friendly, attitude free, positively keen for newcomers to join in, and truly evangelical about the potential laptop performance has for artists of all kinds. Go, and bring your laptop!

(At present there are no plans for the laptop jams to return to London, but they're still very active in the Brighton area – see their website for the latest news. Filmmaker Richard Harris has produced a 24-minute documentary called 'Laptop Jam', which (and I quote) 'captures the LTJ experience with a fast-paced blend of live performance footage, surreal interviews and warped images.' At the time of writing there are no arrangements for distributing this film, but if you're interested you can contact Richard via www.bigbamboo.org.uk.)

Studio special

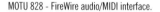

As stated previously, I've opted to take a pretty hard line about laptop-friendly gear – I maintain it has to be bus-powered. Once your laptop is tethered to a mains supply, whether it's at home, in the studio, or in a hotel room, then you can hook it up to the same gear that everybody else uses. There are a few gadgets though, which are popular with laptop users because of their portability, even if they still need a wall wart to get 'em going!

The MOTU 828 (www.motu.com) is very popular – it must have been the first FireWire-based audio interface on the market, and a lot of people snapped it up, despite its clunky rack-mount format and need for mains power. I nearly bought one myself, but I held out for a bus-powered interface, and sure enough, M-Audio came up with the FW410. The 828 is still a tempting proposition though – with up to 20 inputs and 22 outputs (including 8-in/8-out analogue, 2 mic/guitar, and optical connections), MIDI in/out, and standalone mixer functions. The 828 is an ideal way to bridge the 'old' and 'new' worlds of music technology.

MOTU 828 - FireWire audio/MIDI interface.

- *I use a MOTU 828 mainly, just in stereo mode for live. With the dancefloor stuff I've got I might start breaking it out into a mixer. I use it because the sound quality is noticeably better, also because if you're doing a dance music set in a club and they've got a pair of knackered 1210s that have been taken*

apart and maintained over the years and somebody's left the shields out of the motors and you try setting up a laptop with a mini jack stereo out next to a pair of 1210s that's powered up, you get the most insane transformer squeal. The cheap FireWire stuff is starting to come out, but my MOTU will never go out of style! J-Lab

The Presonus FireStation (www.presonus.com) is broadly similar to the MOTU 828 – a rack-mounted unit, tragically mains powered, with FireWire connectivity – the main difference being the FireStation's support for the mLAN communications format developed by Yamaha (Music Local Area Network), which should enable seamless high-speed communication between computers and music hardware via FireWire.

M-Audio's Quattro (www.m-audio.com) is a 4-in/4-out USB audio interface (plus MIDI in/out). The Quattro is VERY popular with laptop users because it's affordable, because it sounds good, because it's USB, and because it's physically small. Of course the negatives are mains power and USB, though if you're using a computer without FireWire then your options are limited. The Quattro is an interface – it lacks some of the more comprehensive mixer-type functions found in units such as the 828 and FireStation, but of course they are far more expensive!

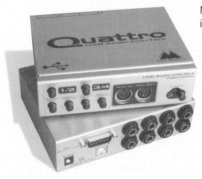

M-Audio's popular Quattro USB audio/MIDI interface – but it needs a wall-wart!

- *It's the Quattro. It is just what it says, its a 4-in-4 out audio capture device. People forget that it doesn't actually have mixer controls, because it's designed to be used with a mixer. You do need to run it off the mains, though I find that works better with the low spec laptops I use, because it doesn't drain the battery. It also has MIDI in and out.* IriXx

TC Electronic's PowerCore Firewire (www.tcelectronic.com) is a high-end rack-mount effects processor which appears as a VST or AudioUnit plug-in inside host computer apps. For some reason it always appears in ads alongside swanky laptops like the PowerBook, but its need for mains power and the unportable 19 inch rack design don't really lend it to laptop use. Once again, I think people mistake 'FireWire' for 'laptop'...it's great for when you take your laptop in the studio, but alas, you can't take it with you...and you probably can't afford it, anyway.

There are more: RME's Multiface (www.rme-audio.com) is an interface option for users with PC Cardbus slots, very high-end. Edirol (www.edirol.co.uk) are always showing new USB-based audio/MIDI interfaces (now including USB2), but their

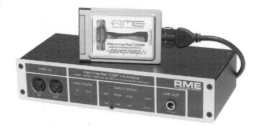

RME Hammerfall DSP Multiface with
Cardbus.

reluctance to embrace FireWire seems to have restricted them to quite basic USB-bus powered devices; their mains powered boxes are more fully-featured; insert usual USB audio caveats – again!

I talked about the M-Audio Oxygen8 (www.m-audio.com) earlier; it's a well-designed USB-powered keyboard/controller. Well, it has a cousin – the Ozone, which in simple terms adds audio interfacing to the Oxygen8 format. I thought the Ozone looked really cool, but I was crushed when I discovered it was mains powered only. It would be good if at least it had an 'Oxygen8' mode, where it could act as a keyboard/controller on bus-power. If you've got more cash, and the right connections on your laptop, I would recommend sticking with M-Audio, but going for the Oxygen8 and the FW410. Still, if you are in the market for a mains powered keyboard/controller/interface combo, the Ozone is a good bet.

M-Audio Ozone – unfortunately it's mains powered only

The best reason for using your laptop in the studio is that you can plug into some quality monitor speakers, and connecting your computer to an external screen. As long as you've got a decent audio interface, then speaker-related matters aren't really any different than for any other studio, so not for this book. But if your laptop will support it, plugging into a large screen has real benefits. Some computers only support mirroring, which is what it's called when you see the same image on both screens – this isn't so useful as dual display or expanded desktop mode, which lets you spread your apps across both screens, or maybe just spread one space-greedy app over the two. I think more laptop users are going to start working like this – instead of keeping a separate desktop computer, they will simply bring back the laptop, and plug it into a home setup consisting of a display and speakers. There is a longer history of dual display use amongst video makers and graphic designers, but musicians are starting to do it more. With the popularity of Rewire, and the ease with which separate apps can be synced, screen space is suddenly in greater demand, and since version 2, Reason supports dual displays; although most of its features are confined to the virtual rack system, the sequencer window can be detached from the rack and opened out onto a second monitor. I've worked like this a couple of times, and it felt good, nice'n'roomy!

Adding video

- *The inherent problem with laptops live and the whole computer live thing is that it doesn't have a visual element, there's not a lot for the audience to latch onto. It's always a worry that it's more entertaining for the person playing than it is for the audience, and you've got to have a kind of focus for the audience which demonstrates that you're actually doing something, cos a lot of the time you might as well be miming, and people think you're miming, and that does happen – we've all done it! No-one's any the wiser either way, so if you can demonstrate some sort of interface which proves that you're kind of doing something, I think as an audience, I know I appreciate it.* Pendle

- *It's good that people are doing it on stage rather than doing it over an internet connection; it's good they're out there. The first person I saw use just a laptop live was Aphex Twin – he had female body builders in fetish gear dancing to all these beautiful ambient tunes while he laid on the floor with a cigar, doing stuff at a laptop.* J-Lab

- *As soon as you're on stage, as soon as people pay money to see you on stage, then I think you have to deliver something visual. If you're a singer then it should be...you; but if all you've got is a laptop then you need to come up with something else.* mindlobster

- *You've got to be careful of being lazy really; anybody can sit there and make a racket, but if you expect anyone to get anything out of it, or experience it in the way you want them to, you've got to do more than just look at the keyboard.* Pendle

What is this chapter about?

Visuals. Eye candy. Things to look at on stage. It's about deciding if you want to give your audience some visual interest.

- *I think some theatrical component is always good in a live setting – otherwise you may as well be listening to a recording.*

  I was asked to play a music festival not long ago, but ended up not doing it when the organiser found out I'd be playing from a computer. 'What will the audience be able to see?' he asked. And that struck me as strange, because fundamentally what can the audience see when somebody is sat playing a guitar or a piano?

113

Most recently we used these large brass instruments and lots of movement. If you look like a lunatic you evoke visual interest, so if you look like a lunatic and have these really funny big golden instruments making this beautiful racket, you've got it sorted. Ergo Phizmiz

Laptop music is great fun to do; it's computer music on location, immersive, absorbing. It draws you in – start jamming away, and next thing you know an hour has passed. But what about your audience? Their eyeballs have needs too – visual stimulation is required. It could be anything – other musicians, small animals, jugglers, but what I'm talking about here is the parallels between laptop music and video projections. Although not everybody seems to think so, gigging with a laptop can be about *entertaining* the audience. Yes, I know it's difficult to grasp – a lot of laptop musos treat gigs as something akin to playing on a Game Cube or XBox in front of a paying audience, without even letting them see the screen! It's a cop out – it's dull to watch.

There's a school of thought that says laptop musicians should be anonymous, they should keep their heads down and let the music do the talking. This is a fine purist attitude, but unfortunately it's not fun to watch. No matter how good you sound, you'll discover that audiences appreciate you more if you have a performance element to your show – and for laptop musicians the answer can be right under their nose; turn your computer into a visual asset, not a liability.

• *Laptop musicians are incredibly boring to watch. So unless the people are unusually fascinating it helps to have visuals. I almost always do video or collaborate with a video artist.* Luke

VJing has grown in parallel to the laptop music thing. If you go to Laptop Jams at Brighton, or one of their London shows, you'll see that people are just as excited about video as music. You should try VJing, it's fun, it might make you think differently about your own live music performances, and if nothing else it will make

Arkaos showing the MIDI keyboard window.

MotionDive.

you better-informed when it comes to relating to VJs; perhaps for when you're discussing ideas about a collaborative event. If you get into it, maybe you could begin a whole new parallel VJ career, but if you're *really* adventurous – if you like to live dangerously, you can do music *and* video simultaneously.

If you're using a laptop to make music, then you already have the means of creating visuals too. You can produce images using graphics applications, or you can use a camera. Almost any camera will do – negatives and prints can be scanned, and digital cameras and camcorders can be connected via USB or FireWire. And there are several VJing apps, such as Arkaos (www.arkaos.net), MotionDive (www.motiondive.com), Videodelic (www.uisoftware.com), and VDMXX (www.vidvox.net) which will let you project your videos in an interactive and entertaining way. Running a VHS tape in the background is no longer acceptable!

VJ interview – Agent Simon (www.agentsimon.com)

I use a laptop to do video because it saves my back. I used to use four Kodak projectors and two 16mm projectors when I toured with Test Dept – it took four of us to lift the flight case it fitted in. Now I can take everything in a rucksack. I have been using one free piece of software since 1999, Image/ine (www.image-ine.org). It allows an awful lot of creative input as all the parameters are assignable to the keyboard, mouse or MIDI controller. It allows me to mix three different images/video but it only runs in Mac OS9, so this last year I have invested in Isadora which is another excellent program, as it runs in OS X. Isadora (www.troikatronix.com/izzydownload.html) is a patch-based program so the VJ has to build their own mixer to their own spec. I recently used it at the Brighton beach Laptop Jam as I had problems with Image/ine. I had to make the patch during the show as my hard drive crashed at the last minute and I had to run Norton on it to get it back – anyway it worked a treat. The great thing about Image/ine and Isadora is their flexibility, which truly frees the user to be more creative than most VJ packages with their boring preset effects.

Video capture and editing

Video capture and editing is an art form. It's a whole book in itself, but that does-n't mean you should find it intimidating; it's easier than the 'professionals' would have you believe.

Collecting video material for use in a VJ set is quite unlike preparing for a video shoot or a movie. You should think of it as a parallel to audio sampling. Just as in audio sampling you can bring together material from different sources, different sample rates and resolutions, so in VJing you can draw material from TV, rental videos or DVDs, webcams, JPEGs, DV tape, and digital cameras. It's all good; as with audio sampling, there is virtue in low-res source material!

Getting video from digital stills cameras

You don't have to use a DV camcorder to shoot movies for your projections. Many of the digital stills cameras on the market have a movie mode of some sort; a feature which will let them shoot low resolution video clips – usually quite short, depending on how much memory the camera has, and with a low frame rate. These little movies can work great for video projections, where the video usually has to be compressed anyway, and short, looping, clips are exactly what you want. Some of the cameras even allow basic cutting, copying and deleting – in theory you could shoot and edit movie clips inside your digital camera, move them to your computer, and open them immediately in Arkaos – no video software needed! Once you've spent some time working with one of these cameras, and you've got used to how it behaves, and how its images look when projected, you'll find it easy to judge what material is going to work on the big screen.

Because you don't need the advanced editing features required for 'professional' TV production, you can successfully work with 'consumer' video editing applications like iMovie on the Mac platform, Windows Movie Maker on XP, and Avid Free DV (for Mac and PC – www.avid.com) – all of these are free, so you needn't put out a lot of cash to get started. Maybe you can borrow a camera too.

Avid Free DV – free video editing for Mac and Windows.

I've been talking about how barriers are breaking down between recording, composition, and performance in electronic music, and there's also a shift in the relationship between music and video – this is one of the most positive developments to arise from the use of computers in music. This change is manifesting itself in software – Final Cut Pro, Apple's high-end video editor, now comes bundled with SoundTrack, an Acid-style application optimised for working on...soundtracks (also now available separately), Metro (covered earlier in this book) has some basic video editing options, and applications such as Arboretum's Hyper Engine A-V (www.arboretum.com) and Sonic Foundry's Vegas (www.sonicfoundry.com) might be described as media editors, rather than 'music' or 'video' apps.

- *No one understands it when you press a QWERTY key. They can understand if you have a piano keyboard and you press that. A visual aspect would greatly enhance an electronic music performance.* Lionel Valdellon

Arboretum Hyper Engine A-V

Hyper Engine A-V is an OSX-only development from Arboretum, better known to musicians for their audio plug-ins. Judging from their website, and its low price, HE A-V is being promoted as a step-up for the iMovie user, although such a description would be selling this interesting looking app short.

Like iMovie, HE A-V captures video direct from a DV camcorder or deck, but it will also import numerous video formats from your hard drive. Audio can be recorded or imported, without the need for an associated video track. A selection of plug-ins are included, and it's possible to purchase HE A-V with a larger set of Arboretum plug-ins. Multiple audio channels are supported, and there were no problems getting it to work with the FW410 FireWire audio interface.

The most interesting thing about HE A-V is its interface; video, audio, text, and stills are all displayed in one large window, and can be simply dragged and dropped

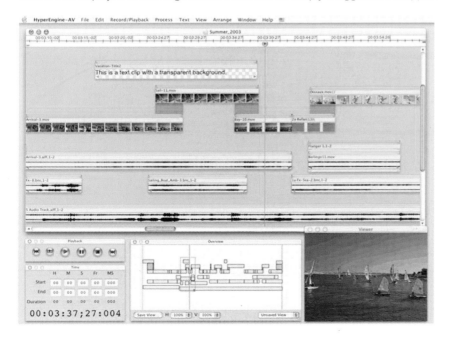

Hyper Engine A-V - media editor with very open interface.

into place anywhere on the timeline. The unfussy interface and the fact that external hardware isn't required make HE A-V a good candidate for laptop work; especially on a laptop with a large screen. Keyboard shortcuts enable the user to zoom in and out quickly, and there is an interesting overview window, quite like the one in Ableton Live, which lets you drag around and zoom in on the viewing area. Usefully, various views can be saved for future recall, make it fast and easy to navigate larger projects. Individual tracks can also be collapsed and expanded to further assist screen management.

Hyper Engine A-V has only a few video effects, and doesn't have a lot of fancy high end video editing features – for that you will need more upmarket software: Avid, Premiere, Final Cut et al. Its strength lies in its simplicity and immediacy, and the way it lets you treat audio, video, and graphics without discrimination. It will accommodate them all on the same track, so you can layout your material in whatever way you like to work.

Great as Final Cut Pro is, and speaking as a 'musician' myself, I rarely need that kind of video editing firepower; even when I'm working on paying video jobs (which does happen once in a while) I prefer to use something simple whenever possible. The expansiveness of HE A-V's working area makes a welcome change from the claustrophobic spaces of 'traditional' editing apps.

Hyper Engine A-V is another futuristic product with a great interface that thinks different (to coin a phrase)…joining Melodyne, Cre8, and Live. The main problem I can see for it is that Arboretum need to give iMovie users enough reasons to 'upgrade'.

Make it easier for your computer

When you're exporting your edited clips from iMovie, or Hyper Engine A-V, or Movie Maker, think about what use you're going to be putting the clips to. You should trim as much fat from the files as possible – this will help Arkaos (or your other VJ app) deal with them more efficiently, and will use less of your computer's resources. Image size – 640x480 is big enough! Frame rate – 15fps is high enough! Keep your clips short. Pre-render effects if possible to free resources. Yeah, you see, it's just like working with audio!

Info

VJ Guineapigguano – 50% of the Petslayer duo, laptop-based audio-visual performers (www.homepage.mac.com/underwoodaudio/disgrace)

VJ interview – VJ Guineapigguano

Petslayer came about because, throughout my life, mostly in my childhood but extending into my adulthood as well, a lot of my pets have somehow met sticky ends!

It was originally going to be a huge graffiti project, but suddenly the space was no longer available, so we put together Petslayer, an audio visual performance thing in which I work on the visuals while wearing funny headgear!

I use video projections because predominantly I'm a visual artist, that's what I like and I personally find it very exciting to see the way that sound and visuals affect each other. I chose to use a laptop instead of video hardware because it was available at the time, and also because it's very portable and versatile – and cheaper.

The first time I went out and performed, I used a very old PowerBook with a broken catch on the lid, that wasn't really much use for anything else. I downloaded a free demo of Videodelic, and there was no way of projecting the images from the PowerBook; the s-video output was broken somehow, I don't remember exactly, I haven't got that

PowerBook any more. The projector couldn't connect to it, so I actually ended up pointing a camcorder at the screen of the laptop and projecting the image from the camcorder. The interesting thing about that was that several people came up to me and said how much they liked that lo-fi look, seeing the borders of the laptop screen, and of course I ended the gig by closing the lid of the laptop, which made a nice shot on screen!

Currently I'm using an iBook with Arkaos. I'm using Arkaos now because it works with Mac OSX. Arkaos has a different look, and it's quite versatile. In some of the Petslayer stuff I want to show a whole short film and have it on one key, and with others I wanted it to respond to the beat of the music, and then also you can just trigger specific things at specific times; there was a specific image I wanted to trigger at certain times and have control over.

I'm using the iBook because it's available! I much prefer Macs; I just think they look much nicer, I feel more comfortable with them generally. I've used them more. The first thing I learned on was a Mac and even though I do use a PC regularly in my day job, I still prefer to work on the Mac whenever I possibly can.

Arkaos

Once you've got your visuals together, you need a way of presenting them live – Arkaos (www.arkaos.net) is perfect for this. If you're familiar with Ableton Live, then it helps to think of Arkaos as the visual version of Live.

Arkaos, which runs on Windows and Mac OS, will import photos, movies, graphics, or Flash movies, which can then be drag'n'dropped across your qwerty keyboard with the trackpad assigned to sending MIDI controllers for effect parameters; or to a MIDI keyboard. Effects work the same way – effect icons are dragged to a key, and they can be alone on a key or share a key with an image. If they are sharing with a visual they obviously take effect on that image or movie loop, but if they are alone then they will take effect on whatever other visual is playing at the time. The Ableton Live parallels continue with automation – start the record option, and your Arkaos performance will be recorded. It can then be rendered to disk as a QuickTime movie for editing in a video application, or reimporting into Arkaos for more manipulation.

Arkaos works on the MIDI principle of synths programs and patches – each synth has up to 128 patches, corresponding of course to MIDI numbers. Arkaos also syncs to MIDI clock, and has a beat detection mode, where different images are triggered according to the beat of incoming audio (as long as your laptop has a mic).

Arkaos justifies its place in a laptop book because of its self-contained nature. Just add a PowerBook and you're ready to gig. I have done this a few times, providing visuals for bands, arriving at the venue with nothing more than a laptop, plugging into the venue's video projector, and jamming away with the band. It always goes down well, and as long as you try to complement the band's on-stage activities instead of bombarding them with your works of video excess, they will be happy.

A lot of computers only mirror their displays when attached to a video projector, which is good if it's all you can do, but it means that everything visible on your screen will be projected at extra large size! if your computer supports monitor spanning, you can use the video projector as a separate display for the main output, and view your Arkaos windows and menus on the laptop screen. It's a bit more discreet, and easier to hide if/when you make any mistakes!

Earlier versions of Arkaos had a lot of stability problems, and there have been times when I've soundchecked, set up the video projections, and then reappeared on stage a few minutes later to find a frozen computer – Arkaos used to have a nasty habit of unregistering itself, which was serious because unregistered versions of Arkaos don't work with MIDI! I would like to stress that Arkaos is now a far more stable beast, and I only mention these problems as examples of things to beware of with performance software in general – make sure you know your system's 'quirks' before you get up in front of an audience.

There is a downloadable demo, and there's a cheaper non-MIDI version of Arkaos called Arkaos VMP, as well as a plug-in version for MP3 players, called Arkaos Visualizer. Arkaos isn't as trippy as some other VJ apps, and it takes a while to get your own style going – the effects are slightly limited in terms of editability, but Arkaos is the best thing out there if you want MIDI/musician oriented control over your visuals. Try it!

VJ Tips

- If you're working with a band, don't swamp them with your visuals, unless you know they want it that way.
- Add site-specific visuals – reflect the venue or event in your images.
- Text is good to use.
- Get more mileage from short video loops by layering them on each other – experiment with transparency.
- If you can, use a laptop that supports dual displays – not mirroring!
- Protect your gear – don't take your eyes off your laptop.
- Do some free gigs to get experience and make connections.
- Get a *very* long VGA lead (20 metres is good) to connect your laptop to the projector – it gives you the freedom to put your projector anywhere in the club.
- In small venues, you can use a king size bed sheet as a projection screen.
- Don't use gaffa tape to suspend your screen/sheet; it takes the venue's paint off the walls and they might not like it. Yes, this has happened to me...

Display spanning workarounds

There are some laptops which will can run in dual display mode, but the feature has been disabled by the manufacturer for marketing reasons (to differentiate between particular models and prices). Notice I'm naming no names. Well, it's possible with some of these computers to do a software hack which re-enables dual display mode – very useful. There is a lot of information about this on the internet, if you care to look. *But* once you start hacking your computer you might invalidate any guarantees/warranties that may be in effect. This is definitely an 'at your own risk' situation – there is great potential for screwing things up!

- *I've got too many other things to look at on stage without wondering if the eye candy I'm producing is any good or not.*   J-Lab

Webcams on stage

Most VJ apps will accept a live feed from a video camera – Arkaos will take video from USB or FireWire. All you do is select the icon for a connected camera in the Streaming Video list, and drag it to a qwerty key like any movie or image, and hit the key when you want to see the feed on screen. Effects can be applied to the feed in real time. These are good ways for getting 'atmospheric' visuals (depends on what the gig looks like); it just adds a little extra something, and proves to the audience that there's some real-time work going on. Use a FireWire camera if you can, you'll get better image quality. I use the Stealthfire, a FireWire camera from Irez; they also make USB cameras (www.irez.com).

Irez Stealthfire – FireWire webcam.

• *There used to be three of us in this old band of mine, we'd be taking out rackfuls of gear and a mixing desk. People would be walking into the nightclub, there's a DJ playing, they're dancing and looking at our gear and saying 'ooh look there's going to be a band on later', they're getting into it. You come on stage – they stop dancing! I used to hate that, we've got nothing interesting to watch here, we've got a bank of electronic equipment – it's not as if were going to be doing guitar solos; we're not the Jimi Hendrix Experience, it's fucking boring. The first time I went out and did a dance gig with my laptop, I sat in the DJ booth just off to the side. The DJ crossfaded from his set into my set; no-one stopped dancing. After about 25 minutes people noticed that there was no DJ standing behind those decks. To me I'd achieved exactly what I set out to do. I'm there to make people dance, I don't want them to watch me, I want them to get off on it. If not then I've failed.* J-Lab

VJ interview – Desaint (www.kinoray.com)

I've been working on the VJing scene for about a year now, going to clubs and setting up shows with my partner Ravi Chandwani . Audiences have been anywhere from 500 to 2000 people in a club environment; my ideal music to VJ to is breakbeats. I describe myself as someone who's still exploring the work, almost like an artist, but like a student as well, learning all the time. It's all based on experimental expression. I'm a lecturer in graphic design, and VJing got me interested in actually showing some of the work that I've done in the past.

I use programs like MotionDive (www.motiondive.com), Final Cut Pro (www.apple.com) to edit the video, and After Effects (www.adobe.com). I use Flash (www.macromedia.com) if there's any branding involved in terms of the club's logo – they ask for that sometimes, or if there's a theme for the evening, I'll do some animation in Flash to support the theme; each set is customised to the event – I have a core library of movie clips that I use all the time, but that will change according to if it's drum and bass, or house music , or even ambient – different moods.

I like using MotionDive because it gives me the feeling that I'm in almost a DJ's environment. I've got two screens, and I can cross fade between the two. I've got a range of different layered effects that I can apply to the video and the Flash, and when you use layers of Flash and video together you can set up some masking techniques which come across really clean. Flash movies look clean and sharp and slick and aren't pixelated at all. It's good software, but its very processor heavy, so you do get dropping of frames.

I'd like to be able to move the video forwards and backwards in a scratch motion and have full control over it. You need to develop some hardcore software to do that. I want to get hands on, I want control! I think there is hardware that will do that, but I don't think its affordable; that's something for the future.

I use a PowerBook because it supports dual monitors, and also for the fact that it looks good! it needs monitor spanning, otherwise you're going to have people seeing your mixing setup.

I can't afford a projector – clubs hire them out for me. It's nice hiring projectors because you can set the specs – otherwise sometimes you just get low level standard projectors which don't have a very strong signal. Resolution problems are common with projectors, this is why I like to rent projectors that I know will have the right resolution settings.

At big events I will use two Macs, it's a safety thing, they both have the same library. I don't use a mixer, just a switcher box to switch between them.

A lot of the time I'll show only certain visuals that relate to the DJ's music – setting the mood is very important. So far it's all been positive and supportive; the DJs will come up and say 'thanks for putting on that great show'; I would like to work more closely with DJs in the future – working on sets in advance of the gigs.

Just enjoy what you're creating. Don't think 'I must be careful not to use this', just go out and be expressive, do what you wanna do. If it's a very subtle pornography, it can come across as nice imagery, or if it's politics involved, and you're trying to display a message, don't be afraid of showing it. You're the one who's putting across a performance. It's an art form. At the of the day you're not getting paid much as a VJ, sometimes you're not getting paid at all. You're doing it purely for the love of it, so people are going to have to bite the bullet and accept what they get.

I like to think about an event – what kind of music they're going to be playing – and build my content around that. I do use music software myself, and that makes me more sensitive to understanding build-ups in music, so I can bring people higher in a visual sense when the music comes up.

i would love to run music and video at the same time, but I haven't found the right software yet, and when the time comes I'd like it to involve performance by at least 4 or 5 other musicians or artists.

In the future I'd like to see more dynamic screen layouts – more clever ways of using screens in a particular environment.

Jamming with music and video – at the same time!

This is where the 'living dangerously' that I mentioned earlier comes in. You can get great results by running Ableton Live and Arkaos at the same time. This gives you a very strong connection between the sound you're making and what people are seeing on screen – you can choose whether to conform to a pre-planned set list, or you can jam and improvise with sound and vision at the same time. This is way cool, and actually isn't too demanding of your computer. I have done this stunt with an old PowerBook G4 400MHz – having the maximum amount of RAM is more important than having the latest and fastest processor. It can also be done across two laptops (if you're lucky enough to have access to two) – and I'll describe that method too. I'm sure other people have different ways of doing it, and with different apps, but this is what I do and it works!

With one laptop

You need one laptop with as much RAM as possible, and a MIDI/USB keyboard. I use the aforementioned PowerBook G4, 400Mhz with 384MB of RAM, and the M-Audio Oxygen8. You don't have to use a PowerBook, but it does have to be a computer that supports dual display mode.

Prepare your set in Ableton Live as usual. Remember that you're going to be dealing with two things at once, so you have to make things a little simpler for you and for your laptop. Pre-render any effects that you don't need to tweak during your gig. Try to reduce the number of tracks. Where possible, mix stereo clips to mono, and reduce sample rates on any clips where you don't think it will be audible. If you've got any long clips where you're only using a small portion, open your audio editor and trim away the excess, making a smaller file.

Enter MIDI Map mode (command/m), and play the Oxygen8 to assign MIDI notes to the scenes in your Live set, using channel 1. If you have more than one song in the same Live file, change to channel 2 and repeat the process (then channel 3 and so on if necessary). If you have any effects in the Live set, assign MIDI controllers to them that correspond to the numbers used by your keyboard's knobs or faders. Exit MIDI Map when you're finished.

When you build your Arkaos set, make sure you use the MIDI keyboard mode (click the icon at bottom left of the patch window). Use a separate patch for each song in the set – you can give the patches the same names as the songs they relates to. You don't want to push your computer too hard, so try to use small movie and image files. If there's any unwanted audio associated with the movie clips, delete it.

When you've added your effects to the keyboard, double click them to access the assignable MIDI parameters. Use MIDI controller numbers that correspond to the numbers used by your keyboard's knobs or faders.

When you've got your Live and Arkaos sets ready, and open on screen, you should check to make sure your computer isn't running anything in the background that it doesn't need. Reduce the size of the Live and Arkaos windows so you only see the essential elements of each app. Play some notes on the MIDI keyboard – you should hear a scene trigger in Live, and see a corresponding visual in the Arkaos preview window. If your laptop is connected to a projector or second monitor, you can go into Full Screen mode and see your video output on the external monitor.

Play with the knobs/faders on your keyboard – you should see some change to the effects parameters in Arkaos and hear some change to the effects in Live (this may be too literal a relationship between the effects for you, in which case it's easy to setup the effects differently).

When you get to the end of your first song, you need to send a program change from your keyboard, so that Arkaos will load the next patch, and, if you have several songs in your Live set, you will need to send a channel change too. The procedure for this varies on different keyboards – it's a little faster on the Evolutions than on the M-Audios.

That's pretty much it. You need a lot of RAM, and you need to accept that you're compromising on the performance of each app to benefit the whole. When it comes together, and works as you planned, it's great, and audiences love it.

With two laptops

This is pretty much the same as above, but by spreading your resources over two computers, you can go a little further with the number of things happening at once. The only extra gadget you need for this to work is a simple 1x MIDI to 1xUSB interface, such as Edirol's UM-1 (www.edirol.co.uk), or M-Audio's Uno. Connect the keyboard to one of the laptops as usual via the keyboard's USB out, then use the UM-1 (or...) to connect the keyboard's MIDI output to the second laptop's USB port. The Oxygen8 has a MIDI port which supports this, as do the Evolution MIDI/USB keyboards – you'll have to check with other brands.

I've used these set-ups for several gigs, and have never experienced a crash or any other problem – advance planning pays off! If you feel you need more interaction with Live, then just map some individual clips to MIDI notes that aren't also controlling scenes or Arkaos images, so that you can jam with these. Arkaos can be pretty much left to its own devices if you've set it up properly – you don't need to keep checking it (but once in a while it's probably a good idea).

There are other ways to configure Arkaos – you can use it with a sequencer (hardware or software), because it receives MIDI clock and, following a recent update, has ReWire too. I don't think that linking Arkaos to a sequencer would be so interesting for live use, but it could create very interesting situations in the studio.

At the venue

Once you have your video material sorted out on your laptop, there are still other practical problems to deal with. Like projectors and screens. If you're doing a 'better' class of venue, then they might have an installed video system – a lot of clubs have something along these lines, but it's not so common in 'music' venues. Sometimes the promoter will cover the cost of hiring a system, but again, that depends on the quality of the gig. Often it's left up to you to provide the video equipment, so either you can reach into your own pocket to hire, or you better try to make some well-equipped friends.

There are a lot of very small video projectors around, and although they won't deliver spectacularly proportioned images, they are bright and sharp, which is important. You will need the projector to be at a reasonable distance from the stage, to get a good size image, so you may have to be creative about where it

Arkaos

Don't be too reliant on the standard effects – everybody else has them too! Your work will be more distinctive if you base your visual style around the content that you import into Arkaos.

goes. I have put them over fire exits, on top of pizza ovens, on bars, on stools, on other bands' equipment, all over the place. The only limit is the length of your video cable – and you better appoint a friend to act as 'minder' for the projector while you're on stage.

Screens? If you want to, you can buy a fancy free-standing screen. I have used bedsheets, folding projection sheets, and plain old walls, they all work in a way – it doesn't have to be a cinema-quality experience.

If you're appearing with another band/performer who's also using video, then you can pool your resources – this saves carrying more gear, money, and set-up time. Combine your screens to make a bigger projection area, share the best quality projector between you, or use both projectors at once – very cool!

Fogscreen – strange but true.

Projecting video in a live environment, where you don't have the ideal situation, can be done very successfully. Some nights you will get better results than you could have dreamed of, with perfect placement for screen and projector, and a huge, sharp, image; other nights you will get a murky, TV-sized smear on the wall and be glad you got that. And *remember* to make sure the lights are going to be low when your set starts, otherwise nobody will be able to see your work anyway.

And, while we're talking about screens and 'ideal situations', take a look at the Fogscreen (www.fogscreen.com), a screen made of 'fog', which you can walk through. It's not a joke, this has great potential for performance use.

- *I don't think it's boring to watch a music performance done by a lonely guy with a laptop, because it's the listening experience that matters. On the other hand I don't mind having things to look at during a gig, but very often the outcome is more a VJ thing than a closely related artistic valuable creation. I like it when there's a connection between the two. If this is impossible for some reason, I'd rather play in the dark.* Eavesdropper

iSociety interaction – that's what laptops are for

Buy a desktop computer and kiss the world goodbye. Buy a laptop and there's no excuse – you can be out there every day, interacting with your environment and other people. It could be a cafe – that's usually where I end up (betraying my personal interest in all things caffeine-related); it can be a friend's house, the beach, the park, the pub (careful), or any suitable public space. In theory, a quiet studio or room at home should be the ideal creative environment, but it doesn't work out like that. Sitting at a table in a cafe – surrounded by people talking and moving around, probably even with muzak playing in the background – can be more of an inspiration and less of a distraction than all those things to do around the house/studio, like alphabetising your CD collection, or doing your tax returns, or the vacuuming (now that's pushing it).

- *The joy of having a laptop is that you can react to your environment. If you're having a problem with a tune it might not be the software, it might just be where you're sitting. Turn round and face the opposite way...go out ...a friend of mine does a lot of his stuff in a park. To avoid muggers he climbs trees. He's an expert tree climber – he's worked as a tree surgeon for some years; he puts his laptop in a rucksack, climbs twenty feet up a tree where nobody sees him, and sits up there with the thing harnessed to him.* J-Lab

The Brighton/London Laptop Jams illustrate this – anybody who thinks computers have to be insular should go to one of their events.

The laptop DJ

What is this chapter about?

DJing with laptops. How to do it cheap, how to do it expensive, and how it meets music creation in the middle – with some VJing on the side!

A lot of people are interested in the laptop DJ thing. DJing and laptops are both hot at the moment, so anything that combines the two – look out! Old-school/skool/skule DJs are into it, laptop 'musicians' are into it, and people with no previous experience of anything are into it; laptop DJing is an idea whose time has come.

There are many advantages to DJing with a laptop, both practical and creative. No matter which way you're coming at it from, there is a way into it – in terms of equipment and action – that'll suit your way of doing things. A laptop can be used in addition to turntables, or a laptop can be used instead of turntables, as an alternative to lugging around boxes full of vinyl.

DJ software is easy to use; the art of DJing lies in the DJ, not the gear – judging what to play and when, how to relate to an audience; these are things that software doesn't do for you – yet. So beware: just because it's easy doesn't mean you're good at it.

It's hard at times to separate DJing from performance and improvisation and composition. There are few DJ-specific products, it's just about how you use them. Take me, for example. I am not a DJ, but I have used DJ software as part of my live set. Sometimes I do gigs where I'm basically DJing with my own music – keeping it simple while I'm busy dealing with video projections at the same time. Something like NI's Traktor gives me the minimum amount of flexibility and spontaneity I need without demanding too much attention.

DJ software

Good news – not only is DJ software easy to operate, it's easy to get. There are free and cheap DJ apps out there which are perfectly good enough to take on stage. You get what you pay for, they say, but is that true with DJ software? You will have to decide.

And what makes good DJ software anyway? Let's assume that opening a bunch of QuickTime files on screen and playing them one after the other doesn't constitute DJing (though anything is possible). The feature list should include some of these: two or more virtual decks, playlist management, mixer functions, MIDI control, tap tempo, pre-listen, beat detection, filters, EQ...which of these you need and how you prioritise them is your call. The best thing to do is download some demos and try them before you buy.

'Buy'? Sorry, I forgot about those freebies for a minute

DeKstasy (www.sonophile.com), is a Mac OSX-only free DJ app. Although its start-up window prominently features a turntable image, DeKstasy's interface makes no attempt to replicate DJ hardware. Admirable. It simply tells you what you need to know to do the job with as little fuss as possible. I really appreciated this no-frills approach; DeKstasy just looks like part of the Mac OS. Despite a minimalist approach to design, it's well specified. DeKstasy will work with AIF, WAV, MP3, and will take audio from a CD. Any uncompressed formats can be converted to MP3 – all files referred to by DeKstasy can be kept in one central location. You can even record audio directly into it. Playlists (or 'crates', as they call them) can be created, saved, and merged, with support for the ID3 tags on MP3 files – containing track info.

DeKstasy (mixer window) – free DJing for Mac OSX.

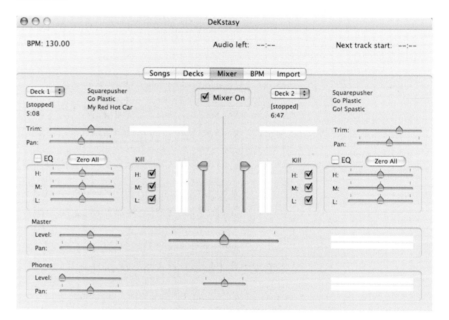

Imported tracks are analysed as DeKstasy finds their BPM, this can be edited if you're not convinced by the results. Songs can be previewed before loading into one of the four decks, and I mean properly previewed – the preview output can be sent to a separate audio output (as long as you're using a suitable audio interface, of course). DeKstasy's ability to detect BPM can also be directed towards external audio, so you can pick up tempo from another sound source; this automated feature can also be used alongside tap tempo. DeKstasy also sends MIDI sync, so other music applications or hardware can be used to add more sounds or instrument parts. There is a mixer with hi/mid/low EQ and kill switches, but there are no filters. There are looping capabilities, but no scratching.

Prelistening

While one song is playing, DJs need to be able to listen to another, so they can cue it – bring it into the mix at a suitable point. This is prelistening, and to do it properly an extra audio output is needed, hence the DJ's interest in audio interfaces.

Even if there were more advanced performance options available, it would be difficult to easily implement them in a performance situation because DeKstasy doesn't support any MIDI control, and has only limited qwerty control. However, Sonophile hope to add MIDI and further qwerty controls soon, and this will make DeKstasy even more interesting. I suggest you check the website – by the time you read this the extra control features may have been added. And it's free. Did I mention that it's free?

And there are other free ones around, all with their own advantages and drawbacks. Mixxx (mixxx.sourceforge.net) comes in all flavours – Mac, Windows, *and* Linux, with MP3s and Ogg Vorbis the audio formats of choice. It looks like a simplistic version of NI's Traktor, with two decks, a playlist, and a mixer. Prelisten and

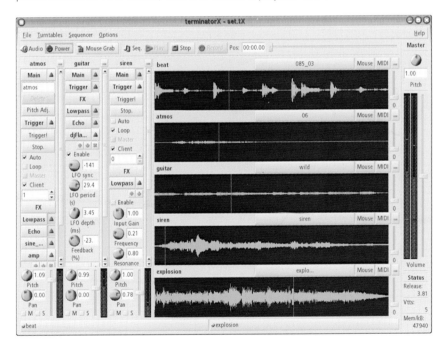

TerminatorX has real-time effects.

MIDI control mapping are supported. In my limited experience of Mixxx I found it excessively system-hungry.

You should also look at GDAM – Geoff and Dave's Audio Mixer (www.gdam.sourceforge.net) for Linux and Mac OSX, and TerminatorX for Linux (www.terminatorx.cx). tX has real-time effects courtesy of LADSPA plug-ins, and scratching via the mouse. It works with many sound formats, including Sun AU, Ogg Vorbis, MP3, AIF, and WAV. I suggest you see Brian Redfern's excellent tX pages at www.djcj.org for the more detailed lowdown on TerminatorX.

Or you can buy them

Then there's the apps you have to pay actual money for, like DJ1800 (www.dj1800.com), which has been designed to emulate the Denon DN-1800F CD player. DJ1800 is well equipped – with 4 decks, pitch shift, support for Griffin PowerMate and ContourDesign Shuttle controllers (www.griffintechnology.com, www.contourdesign.com), mixer, eq, prelisten via multiple sound devices, iTunes library integration, and more. The problem is the interface – it only makes sense if you know the Denon CD decks it's based on. Otherwise it's like the DJ version of those silly music apps that copy rackmount hardware design. It's not a design that's optimised for laptop keyboard use. Still, that's just my opinion – you've probably noticed by now that I have a downer on virtual hardware! Try it for yourself – there's a time-limited demo available for download.

DJ1800 is well equipped – with four decks, pitch shift, support for Griffin PowerMate and ContourDesign Shuttle controllers, mixer, eq, prelisten via multiple sound devices, iTunes library integration, and more.

Traktor

Further up the price ladder – a lot further – is Native Instruments' Traktor DJ Studio (www.nativeinstruments.com). This is perhaps the DJ software with the biggest company behind it, and it shows. Traktor features a file browser (MP3s, AIFs, and WAVs are supported), two virtual decks with waveform display, a mixer with EQ, two filters, and a range of useful looping features. Traktor allows you to record your set to disk for burning mix CDs. As well as working standalone, Traktor will integrate with external hardware such as MIDI controllers and audio interfaces, and there's a special version that works with Final Scratch on Mac OS, Windows, *and* Linux.

I don't like virtual knobs and faders. I don't like virtual knobs and...oh, what's the use? The word 'intuitive' is not in NI's collective vocabulary – they've got their ugly way of doing things and they're sticking to it. After some time I was able to work with Traktor comfortably, but this was *despite* their interface, and with the help

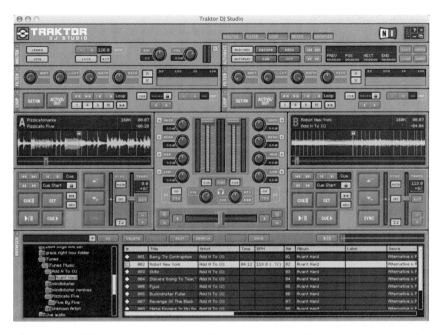

Traktor DJ Studio main window. Traktor features a file browser, two virtual decks with waveform display, a mixer with EQ, two filters, and a range of useful looping features.

of an external MIDI controller. Traktor does have reasonable screen management – it's possible to hide everything but the decks, and for the easily distracted, there's a full-screen option.

As usual with NI products, Traktor is unforgiving of 'old' computers – minimum system requirements for Mac are OS10.2.6, G4 1GHz, 256MB RAM, and for Windows 2000/XP, Pentium/Athlon 1GHz, 128MB RAM. As well as using a PowerBook, I tried to run Traktor on a Key Lime iBook...this failed miserably because Traktor won't work with screen resolutions below 1024x768, so I couldn't even start it! This is the sort of thing you have to deal with if you're trying to use older laptops.

Anyway, assuming Traktor thinks your computer's good enough, when it first runs it can search your hard drive for all audio files, and display them in the searchable browser. This includes any connected drives, removable media, the iTunes library (individual playlists are recognised), and (if you have one) an attached iPod. I had no problems getting Traktor to recognise the FW410 interface when setting it up for prelistening.

The first thing to do is use the browser to load a song into each deck. Traktor has sophisticated beat analysis functions, and these can be supplemented with a beat grid, which enables a high level of accuracy over a song's playback. Up to ten cue points can be created, and up to ten loops can be marked and saved for later recall within each song; their lengths can be manipulated in real time. Songs playing on the decks can be forced to synchronise with each other. Songs (or parts of them) can be played in reverse. Traktor's mixer section features high/mid/low EQ (with kill switches) for each deck. There is a resonant filter section for each deck too. Decks can be told to stop playing at the end of the song, or automatically load the next song. They can be told to reset when new song is loaded, and playing songs can be 'locked', cutting down your chances of embarrassing silences midsong. And yes, you can scratch with Traktor. Just click on the waveform of the currently playing song, and start dragging the mouse around; it feels pretty crude with a laptop trackpad, if you want to develop this I suggest experimenting with external MIDI controllers.

Traktor is well set-up with qwerty keyboard shortcuts for all of its controls – these are already configured, but if you want to set them up a different way, you can. These controls can also be operated via MIDI – this needs to be configured by you. I found the qwerty shortcuts too hard to remember – there's just too many of them! I didn't begin to take Traktor seriously until I plugged in the Evolution UC33. Because Traktor has so many functions, you need a MIDI controller with a lot of knobs and faders – the UC33 is it. I've used it with other applications, most frequently with Ableton Live, but Live already works at a high level with the qwerty controls, there isn't always a case for using a controller too. I found that the UC33 has enough controls on its to surface to operate Traktor without having to go to a second preset, so it was really simple to use, without having to worry about forgetting which preset you were in.

If you're thinking of buying Traktor, you should aim to buy a UC33 to go with it. MIDI keyboard controllers like the Oxygen8 or MK225C or ReMOTE25 work reasonably well with it too, but the piano-style keys are redundant with Traktor – you need knobs and faders and lots of em. At the time of writing, Evolution don't make a template for Traktor, but you can always make your own, or do what I did and label the controls with masking tape and a marker pen. Looks lo-tech but it works fine.

There are times on stage with a laptop when you can feel like a bit of a phoney; nobody knows what you're up to. I've had people congratulate me after a gig and then ask me what I was doing! When the UC33 comes into the picture, you can actually look and feel like you're doing something, even if you're still sending the same old messages to your software. The tactility returns – I believe using a controller affects my sound during a performance because it makes me more inclined to tweak things constantly. When you have a dedicated hardware controller for each function or parameter, it's easier to work with – and you're less likely to make some sort of terminal mistake. Adding the UC33 to Traktor instantly bypassed my reservations about the virtual knobs and buttons – you can use the real ones on the UC33. They are made for each other.

As I said, I'm not a DJ, so I spent very little time scratching, and quickly moved onto trying to use it in a more jammy/performance way. If you use the automatic load feature, you can get together a few dozen/hundred audio clips and set Traktor off running through them in sequence, while you work frantically with the EQ and filters, crossfader, loops and reverse function. You can use speech, sound effects, beats, noise, anything; just set it off and see how they fall together. You could even use Traktor's record function to record the jam, and then write it to disk as a stereo file. Might be an interesting way to get some new sounds for use in other pieces – or it might just be a piece in itself.

Without a UC33, Traktor sucks. With a UC33, Traktor is NI's greatest software to date – I found it a lot more interesting than their synths and samplers. The filters sound great, and are easy to understand. As somebody coming to it from the musician/performer side, I found it much easier to relate to than other DJ apps. I can imagine using it on stage alongside Arkaos, spreading my attention between both apps. In these situations I need a certain amount of interaction with the music, but not too much – Traktor's loops, cues, filters and EQ give me enough control without demanding 100% of my attention.

Beware: Traktor is highly addictive. If you use iTunes you are well and truly stuffed because you're never gonna get any work done ever again – all you'll want to do is play with the integration between Traktor and iTunes.

Why Traktor is good for DJs

Saveable loop/cue features. Automation. Portability. iPod and iTunes integration. File management. The ability to have 1000's of songs on a drive, and access any of them at any time. Scratching, pitch shift, tempo control, beat markers. EQs with frequency kills for lo/mid/hi. High quality filters. Pre listen. Burn your set to audio CD.

Why Traktor is good for musicians

Play back your songs or backing tracks live with automated loading – more interactive than a MD deck. Jamming with loops, filters and EQ. An interesting way of sequencing your CD track listing. Experimental playlists – create random mixes by loading 100s of short clips from your drive and seeing how Traktor moves between them. It's fun – that's a good enough reason.

DJing with Ableton Live

I don't personally feel that Ableton is a good choice for DJing – the interface is far more suited for performance in the instrument sense, and the process of applying warp markers to enable beat matching is too laborious for a lazy guy like me. I like Traktor for DJing, and Live for jamming. However, if your definition of 'DJing' is more fluid, and your set is more about merging original samples, parts, and sounds with the songs, than there could be something in it. At the moment Live doesn't support MP3s, which is another drawback for DJs, as so many other DJ apps do, and the ID3 tags with song/artist information are very useful for playlist functions. However, there's no reason to think Ableton won't add more DJ friendly futures in the future – they've already added a crossfader (Ableton are very good at responding to user pressure for new features – if you have things you want them to include you should start hassling them via their website!).

iTunes DJ

See Chapter 2 for more iTunes info. iTunes works with playlists, and it has a handy soundcheck feature for levelling song volumes; but the only crossfading it does is over a specified length of time between songs, without real-time control or beat matching. DJing with iTunes would be...basic!

iPod DJ

More of the above. Less than a laptop. The only advantage the iPod has is portability, and its ability to hold an obscene number of songs. HOWEVER that doesn't mean a lot of people aren't trying to make it work in a DJ environment. A club called APT (www.aptwebsite.com) in New York has a DJ booth with two iPods and a mixer, where patrons can try their hand at DJing – for seven minutes each. Nowax (www.nowax.co.uk) in London operate a night where iPod owners can come along and compete against each other. I would love to see somebody good do this – I think the options are too limited, unless you add some extra ear candy in the shape of some real-time effects. Korg's Kaoss Pad (www.korg.com) or Alesis' AirFX (www.alesis.com) would be ideal additions to an iPod DJ setup – they both have great interfaces for performing, and don't cost too much! But by the time you add up the cost of an iPod (or two), a mixer, and outboard effects, you might as well buy a laptop, you rich kid you.

iPod DJing at APT in New York.

If you had a venue with a PC or Mac that carried Traktor DJ, that would be different. You could bring your iPod, with the playlist ready to go, and plug it into the computer. This is one of those technological ideas that sounds great, but the reality might be different – it depends on the venue having a well-maintained computer, for one thing.

Final Scratch

Have you seen Final Scratch (www.finalscratch.com)? It's a package which includes three 12 inch vinyl records and a USB/audio interface for your computer. You can put the record on your decks and scratch audio files on your computer. Like Fogscreen, I thought Final Scratch was a joke when I first heard of it – I still get the feeling somebody's pulling my leg. You need two turntables, a mixer, and a laptop. The USB/audio interface, called a Scratch Amp, connects these different elements. Instead of music, the records contain timecode which is transmitted to your computer. At the computer end, Final Scratch uses a basic version of Traktor, called Traktor FS, which lacks some of Traktor Studio's features, such as filters and EQ.

This concept does nothing for me, but if you're already DJing with vinyl, and have all of the necessary hardware, then it might be the best thing since sliced bread; the DJ version of a MIDI/USB controller keyboard, or a guitar synth controller. There's nothing else like it – there's even a CD version for those who use

Alesis AirFX – a good add-on for applying real-time effects.

Final Scratch with DJ and decks.

Scratch Amp close-up.

CD decks, but I can't help but feel Final Scratch is interim technology, and soon, very soon probably, something will come along that gives DJs the same control without being tied to decks and a mixer.

Another thing worth pointing out is that Final Scratch/Traktor FS is available for Mac OS, Windows, AND Linux – so nobody has to feel left out. This might also lead Linux users to wonder if there'll be a full Linux version of Traktor available some time.

Interfaces

There's no need to repeat what's been said in earlier chapters about audio interfaces. Any audio interface that has multi channel outputs will enable prelistening/cueing for DJs. It depends on the individual combinations of software and hardware, nothing should be taken for granted, but these are all interfaces that DJs use: Griffin iMic, M-Audio Quattro, M-Audio FW410, MOTU 828, eMagic 2|6, Gigaport. A new arrival is the Echo Indigo DJ (www.echoaudio.com), another incarnation of the versatile PC card. This version has two separate stereo outputs, so you can send stereo to the mixer, and use the other to feed your headphones for prelistening. As long as your laptop has the required PC card slot, this is one of the most compact and affordable high quality audio interfaces around. It's also useful if your computer lacks FireWire or if you want to keep your FireWire/USB ports free.

Does MP3 sound quality matter?

This is unfortunately a matter of opinion and personal experience over science. All things being equal, it should matter, but in reality..? The music technology world is racing towards lower resolution sounds at one end (the web, streaming, MP3, AAC, etc), and higher resolution at the other (24-bit/96KHz, surround, etc). There are people who will tell you MP3 is fine, there are people who will tell you that you must never use MP3. You should suck it and see – do some gigs with different set-ups, see what happens. But if you are a bad DJ, you have other things to worry about than bit rates!

DJing with VJing

If you would like to try providing your own visuals while doing your DJ set, but are put off because it's too complicated, remember that a lot of VJ apps have beat detection of some sort, so they will react to your beats and rotate through their images automatically. I've use this feature with Arkaos sometimes, and it can work really well. You get a mixture of carefully prepared visuals, with an unpredictable random element and unexpected combinations of effects. Visuals working in this 'automated' way tend to suit being more freeform and, dare I say it, trippy, abstract, because they aren't necessarily going to correspond to the musical structure in the same way as if you're triggering them via MIDI.

Syncing to music apps

DJ apps are beginning to include more facilities for integrating them with other music software, via MIDI clock, or Rewire, as well as including support for MIDI hardware controllers. This is leading to even more crossover between the work of laptop musicians and DJs, which can only be a good thing. It's interesting to see this process going on; there is a lot of talk and coverage about how DJs who get the creative itch are incorporating music making tools, but there's also a lot that musicians can learn from DJ gear – especially those laptop performers who are always looking for new perspectives on live performance.

Everybody talks about 'Professional DJ' tools, this term is meaningless. As with other music equipment, use what works for you; there are cheap (and free) solutions available, and they might be all you need – don't be sold something with a lot of features you don't need just because somebody famous allegedly uses it!

Prelistening without multiple outputs

If you haven't got a multi channel audio interface, but prelistening is really important to you, there are ways of getting it without buying extra hardware – it just takes a little stereo-to-mono shenanigans. With some applications you can assign the master output to mono left, and the prelisten output to mono right, then use a left/right splitter plug to divide the signals as they leave the computer; connecting the prelisten output to your headphones and the master out to the PA. This won't work with Ableton Live, but there is a way...1) Plug a 1/8 inch male stereo to phono dual female adaptor into your laptop's headphone socket. 2) Then attach a male phono to 1/8 inch female stereo adaptor to the right female phono. 3) Connect your headphones to the female stereo output. 4) Connect a single male to two female phono adaptor to the other free female phono. 5) connect this to the PA using a standard stereo phono cable. This sounds messy, and looks ugly busting out of your laptop, but it's cheap and it works. The only drawback is that it turns your stereo output into 'dual mono' – two channels the same. For some users, some styles of music, and some environment,s this doesn't matter, so you will have to decide. I use A LOT of stereo pans in my music, so this would be a last resort for me. (this tip taken from 'DJ-ing Techniques With Live' by Ryan Supak – read the rest of it on www.ableton.com).

No laptop? No problem

What is this chapter about?

Non-laptop portable solutions – things that replace or complement laptops: portable sequencers, samplers, digital recorders, minidisc, mobile phones, PDAs, iPods (yep, them again) – you name it, somebody's out there jamming with it.

If you're interested in portable music making, then you might already have tried, or might be interested in trying, some of the other mobile gadgets out there. Some of them date back to a time when using a laptop wasn't viable, or was just too expensive; while some of them are state-of-the art digital devices – so, as is often the case with laptop music, old meets new in a clash of flying sparks and a faint whiff of scorched circuit boards. None of these are true substitutes for the laptop computer, but some of them are worthwhile companions. Let's get small…

Sequencing

MIDI sequencing, with its independence from the high demands of audio recording and sampling, is the lowest impact form of electronic music composition – because it can work with a simple tone generator, it doesn't ask too much of battery-powered devices. Yamaha (www.yamahasynth.com) started making portable sequencers with the QY10 back last century in 1991. This VHS tape-sized gadget (it actually came in a VHS case) boasted 8-track sequencing, a 6,000 note memory, 76 preset and 24 user-programmable accompaniment patterns, and 30 onboard PCM sounds. For connection to the outside world the QY featured MIDI in and out, and mini jack stereo line out and headphone out.

There are a lot of people making music today whose first taste of sequencing was the QY10; often sometimes in combination with the notorious Novation MM10, a 25-key battery-powered keyboard designed specifically to complement the QY10, even featuring a slot along the top of the housing for the QY to nestle in while performing. The only way to archive songs created on the QY10 was via MIDI, using something like Yamaha's MDF2 or MDF3 data filers, effectively an external floppy disk drive – also battery powered. Primitive as this rig was, I managed to write a lot of songs on the QY10 (one of which endures in my live set) – it was a great machine for getting songs out with the minimum of fuss.

Yamaha MDF3 - portable MIDI/floppy disk data filer.

- *I used to use a Yamaha QY10. I bought one 10 years ago and it was a revelation. It was interesting to be able to knock up loops and beats and then transfer the MIDI files into the Atari.* J-Lab

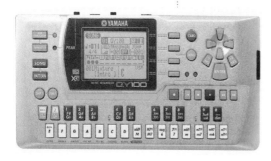

Yamaha QY100 — portable sequencer with guitar/mic input.

Despite the arrival of the fully-functional laptop studio, Yamaha have kept faith with the QY concept. The latest version is the QY100, a 16-track model with 32,000 note memory, 768 preset and 384 user patterns, and 547 voices with 20 drum kits. It also includes effects, smart media storage, 'to host' connector for communication with a PC, and a mic/guitar input, making it possible to use the QY100 as a self-contained studio...just send the output to an external recorder and you've got the whole she-bang. I hope that the QY series will continue, it's so interesting – though I suggest greater computer integration for future models.

Sampling

Although the QYs were (and probably still are) handy for songwriting, they weren't exactly stimulating performance tools (even with the MM10 attached). For live jamming you were better off with something like the SU10, effectively the sampler equivalent of the QY range. Whereas the QYs lacked any performance controls, the SU10 had a ribbon controller strip, usually seen only on more expensive equipment. This could be used to scratch, reverse, and filter one of 48 stored samples. Recording was via a mini jack input, at sample rates from 11.64 – 44.1 KHz, with up to 54 seconds of sample time available depending on the chosen sample rate. Limited though they were, the SU10 perfectly exemplified the 'use what you got' ethic, as people sampled, resampled, mangled and mixed way beyond what you

Yamaha SU200 - battery-powered sampling.

might call reasonable. Entire songs – good songs – have been made using nothing more than the SU10 and a minidisc or DAT recorder.

The SUs also live on, in the shape of the SU200. The control strip remains, and onboard effects and smart-media storage are added, with a couple of knobs for further real-time control. This box isn't going to replace your copy of Gigasampler or HALion or Session, but it's fun – and that's the magic word.

(It's a shame, given Yamaha's contribution to the portable music scene in the past, that they haven't come up with anything exciting for laptop users. USB/FireWire interfaces, or software based on their synths and samplers – or a MIDI controller based on their ribbon controllers. By the way, the RM1x hardware sequencer makes a great control surface for software, although it's not mains powered. Come on Yamaha, how about a USB-powered version of that?!)

Recording

The ever-present minidisc recorder has a part to play here too. MD's value as a recording medium has already been covered, but it can be a jamming instrument in a limited way. Fill an MD with short snippets of sound, the more varied the better, hit shuffle play and listen to the results. *Then* add some sort of real-time external effects unit, such as Alesis' AirFX (www.alesis.com) or Korg's Kaoss Pad (www.korg.com), and you're jamming. This works with CDs too – prepare a CDR with your own loops and clips, and give it a try. If only the Kaoss and AirFx were battery powered it would be perfect!

If you're more interested in jamming or making experimental music, styles where you don't need a carefully-constructed set and synchronisation with other hardware, then you probably could go on stage with one of these simple little gadgets and have a great time – just tell everybody you're using an iPod and they'll accept it without question.

Zoom's PS-02 (www.zoom.co.jp) and Korg's PXR4 are both tiny battery powered digital 4-track recorders with stereo inputs, stereo outputs, smart media storage, onboard effects and editing, virtual tracks, USB connections for computer integration, and best of all, tiny built-in microphones. These could be great for collecting sounds on the fly, doing a little ad-hoc mixing/slicing/processing, and then loading into a computer for further work. They're sold more as jamming (in the guitar sense)/accompaniment tools, but you know, it's not compulsory. It would be nice to record 4 tracks of speech/noise/ambience and process it just using the onboard facilities.

Although these units offer a spontaneous way of recording and experimenting with sound, they still expect you to be using a computer, for USB/smart media archiving. Despite being impressively featured for their size, these boxes don't offer a self-contained composition/recording/performance/distribution solution in the same way that even a basic laptop does.

Grooveboxes

There's a lot of apparent crossover between the laptop and groovebox markets. Devices such as Yamaha's RS7000 and Roland's MC909 have some very desirable laptop music-like features; a combination of MIDI sequencing and sampling, plenty of real-time hands-on control, and (hopefully) solid timing. These are both interesting machines, worth giving space to on stage or in the studio, But they lack the quintessential laptop asset, the thing that makes a piece of gear laptop-friendly or *not* laptop-friendly – battery power; you're not likely to come across anybody jamming in the park with an RS7000.

Mobile phones and PDAs

If you've got a mobile phone that lets you compose ringtones, then you could try using it to create some original tunes. The process can be torturous, but I've done it with a Nokia, and got some interesting sounds, once I re-recorded them into Ableton Live via my laptop's internal microphone, and went to work on them with some EQ and plug-ins. A lot of phones how have audio recording capabilities (some with video), though I don't know how easy it is to get these recorded sounds into a computer afterwards.

There are also music apps for PDAs, including MIDI sequencers, utilities, audio recorders/editors and MP3 players. Most of these are free or cheap, with demos available. They can be fun for experimenting with, but not much use for performance – unless of course you know otherwise.

Yamaha RS7000 – sequencing/sampling workstation with lots of controls.

Sony Clie - now available with built-in video camera and microphone.

Multimedia features are becoming more common on phones and PDAs, they can be much more credible 'data gathering' devices now. As an example, look at the Sony Clie (www.clieplaza.com). MiniMusic (www.minimusic.com) have some nice Palm OS compatible applications – BeatPad (pattern based sequencer), SynthPad (sampler), and SpinPad (graphic sequencer – very interesting). Palm users can also go to www.cix.co.uk/~tralala to grab a free copy of Andy Hunt's Beep – a Stylophone emulator!

GameBoy

Yep. Nanoloop (www.nanoloop.de) is a 16-step sequencer which resides inside a GameBoy cartridge, using the GB's four onboard sound chips as its sound source. 15 patterns can be saved inside a bank to construct a song, and real-time sound editing is possible.

Take your ears shopping

There are a lot of places where you might find inspiring sound gadgets – go to your local toy shop, or kids' section in a supermarket, and see how many electronic noisemaking gadgets they've got – tiny battery powered keyboards and beatboxes, and 8-second voice recording toys; not exactly ProTools, but they are a a lot of fun and can create some interesting sounds. These things are so cheap that even if you only use them once, it'll have been worth the money.

Gadget warning

One of these small boxes isn't enough. People who gig with these things usually have quite a few gadgets strewn across a table, with leads and wall warts (mains adaptors) all over the place...it all ends up being bigger and more complicated than a laptop!

What's next for laptop music?

- *Laptop music has a loooong way to go – so many challenges.* SongCarver

- *I think the future is really in musicians selling DVDs rather than CDs, but even though every major label artist makes videos, they don't package them with the music and there's no portable DVD audio players.* Brian Redfern

What is this chapter about?

Things move fast in laptop music land. This is where I look into my iTealeaves and predict (take a dumb blind stab at guessing) imminent and future developments that will affect laptop musicians. Much as I've been stressing the need to appreciate and enjoy what you have at your disposal now, it's still fun to look forward to the sexy new stuff. And the new bugs. And the new bug fixes. What are the updates, upgrades and innovations that are likely to torment you so cruelly? And what will happen to the activity known as 'laptop music'?

I know what I want. I want more free/cheap software, I want to see different types of people using laptops for music, and in different genres. I want solar power for my laptop (already available from www.aapspower.com). I want to see laptop musicians at the forefront of new forms of music distribution – and this is what other people want:

- *Better paying gigs for electronic musicians.* Lionel Valdellon

- *People giving less attention to equipment and more to music.* Slender Whiteman

- *I'd like to see the extortionate costs of laptops and software coming down so everybody can experience it. I would also like to see the end of copyright so that everything is accessible to everyone. Because it basically is anyway, and to be sampled by someone is surely an honour! Nicking a whole track from someone is a bit silly, but sampling elements is great and it is everywhere. Recontextualising is one of the most interesting areas of modern composition.* Ergo Phizmiz

- *I would like to see tougher laptops. Dells are supposed to be ultra tough, they are also overly heavy; the original curvy rubber-clad iBook was the toughest ever, although hindered by an easy-to-break CD/DVD tray. I should know, I broke it – twice.* mindlobster

You don't need a crystal ball. Many of the advances in laptop technology will be trickle-down from desktops, and incremental improvements to what's there already. Would you consider me a genius if I told you that laptops are going to get faster? No, didn't think so. But that's what will happen, and they will accommodate more RAM, and have more disk space. Faster hard drives are going to appear. USB1 audio interfaces will disappear from the planet like an embarrassing but short-lived rash, replaced by USB2 and FireWire (400 and 800) models. Battery life will increase, perhaps with the benefit of fuel cell technology, allowing charges of up to eight hours. Dual processors will appear on larger models, perhaps with liquid cooling.

Tablets and touch screens

The main constraint on laptop size continues to be the qwerty keyboard. Laptop design would be liberated if somebody could get the tablet thing to work. Some manufacturers, such as Compaq and Acer (www.compaq.com and www.acer.com), have taken some initial steps, but others, like Apple, aren't going for it at all, and there are problems getting people to abandon the traditional keyboard which has worked for so long. At present it's an interesting but unfulfilled direction. It would be great to control Ableton Live by using a touch screen interface, jabbing the screen directly with a finger instead of using any mouse/stylus/keyboard at all – another step closer to playing a 'real' instrument! Screen resolution/definition might be a problem, though, if you have big fingers jabbing at little icons on screen.

If you want to try it, and you got the money, maybe you can. Trolltouch (www.trolltouch.com) make touch screens for desktop and portable computers, including Apple's iBooks. The laptop versions of these screens need to be installed by Trolltouch; you can send them your laptop, or you can buy one from them with the touchscreen pre-installed. I tried to find out if anybody's already using tablets or touchscreens for music, but I couldn't get any information; still, it seems to have potential – well I think so, anyway.

Wireless jamming

In 2002, M-Audio (www.m-audio.com) were talking about Bluetooth-based MIDI products, called MidAir, including adaptors to add wireless MIDI functionality to existing equipment, as well as a range of portable Oxygen8-style keyboards with built-in wireless capabilities. It's not clear what the current situation is with this – M-Audio have gone quiet on the subject, although Kenton (www.kentonuk.com) also have a wireless MIDI system, the Midistream, which works along the lines of existing guitar and bass radio systems.

In theory it's possible to send MIDI over a regular wireless network; you can send MIDI sync from one computer to another without cables or adaptors. It could be a simple and cheap way to do it, if it saves you the cost of buying extra cables and MIDI interfaces. And of course, given our interest in keeping things portable, and carrying a minimum of gear, every cable left at home (intentionally) is a good thing. That's if it works, of course; while it seems tempting to run a cable-free MIDI set-up, it might cause more problems than it solves – yet one more thing to go wrong!

Kenton Midistream - wireless MIDI.

- *The problem with using these types of communication standards is the problem of changing latency. Data transmission is not built for the same real-time usage. It's a bitch, to be honest. I'm always a fan of adapting existing technology, but I'm yet to see anything which could work well wirelessly, except for joysticks and keypads.* SongCarver

In a non-musical context, 'wifi' is the name used to describe wireless networking, and public places where you can access the internet via wifi are called 'hotspots'; it's like an internet cafe, but B.Y.O.C. (Bring Your Own Computer). Sometimes this service is offered free, sometimes it's on a pay basis, whether that's pay per session or subscription – personally, I think it should be free to the public, perhaps funded by the government, or by sponsorship. Paris is developing a city-wide wifi network, and other cities (including Brighton) are said to be following suit.

Wireless base stations can also be used to setup networks at home or in the office – and it's also possible to set up a simple wireless network between two computers without a base station. The claimed range for wireless networking is approximately 150 feet, and Macs and PCs can be networked together.

Getting your laptop ready for wifi is simple and cheap – just add a wireless networking card. Users of recent Apple laptops have a cavity inside their computer for an Airport card; users of other laptops can use the PC Card slot if they have one, or a USB adaptor.

Apple's Airport card

Wifi standards

The official name for the initial wifi standard is IEEE802.11b; this allows data to be sent/received at up to 11Mbps, up to a range of approx. 150 feet. Now there is also IEEE802.11g; known to Mac users as Airport Extreme, with a transfer rate of up to 54Mbps. This standard hasn't been officially adopted by everybody at the time of writing, but Apple just couldn't wait.

Whether wireless networking is of particular interest to laptop musicians remains to be seen, but if you're interested in working on the move with your computer, then it will be relevant to you one way or another. Of course you can use it to perform usual computer related tasks such as checking your e-mail and updating your website, but it will also let you access online sample libraries such as PowerFX (www.powerfx.com) and Sonomic (www.sonomic.com) while you're on the go, so you can grab some beats without having to go home or carry around sample CDs.

Maybe while you're out you could record some sounds, download some samples, integrate them into a new tune, and post it on your website, all without having to go home or plug into the mains or a phone socket!

What's chalk got to do with it?

There's a huge amount of wifi info on the internet, but for UK users at least, there is no single site that gives a clear indication of *exactly* where you will find available hotspots. This is where warchalking comes in – the practice of detecting available wifi networks and informing others of their locations. There are many businesses using wireless networks, and many of them don't seem to know or care that their network can be accessed by outsiders (often literally outside, like sitting on the pavement). In *my* opinion, this is fair game *if* all you're doing is using their network to connect to the internet. But be advised it is actually illegal! However, if you start trying to get into their computers or playing 'funny' tricks with their network, then – *bad idea*. Why is it called 'warchalking'? All is explained at www.warchalking.org!

By the way, can I be the first to call wireless MIDI 'MiFi'?
I thought not.

Controllers
Laptop musicians are obsessed with MIDI controllers! Small boxes with 4 knobs, 61-key MIDI keyboards, fader boxes, mini MIDI mixers such as JL Cooper's CS-32 Mini Desk (www.jlcooper.com). It seems that there is no such thing as the perfect MIDI controller, and the only option is to own several; then it turns into 'which one should I bring tonight?'.

JL Cooper CS-32 Mini Desk - USB MIDI controller.

Quote

People will start to realise that the mouse and keyboard is a stupid interface for making music, and will start to expand into creating their own interface hardware. Luke

The MIDI controller field is now even more open, because there are items of software such as JunXion (www.steim.org), which maps commands sent from any peripheral such as a mouse, or joystick (or other game controller) to MIDI. This means a games joystick, or a mouse, or a graphics tablet, can be used to send program changes, or to change FX parameters...could be fun! And it opens the way to ever more idiosyncratic and individual ways of working, which has to be a good thing.

There's also the build-your-own option – the best place for information on this is www.ucapps.de, where you can see scores of photos and plans for MIDI controllers – though to me there seems little point in building a MIDI controller box when there are more than enough affordable and universally compatible models already available. However, there is room for more adventurous designs. I wonder what other strange devices are out there, or perhaps yet to be built..?

Software

Because it's possible to work in such a self-contained way with laptops, it will be software developments that most define the future of laptop music. A laptop can run the latest versions of software which has been around for many years, and there are also a ton of plug-ins out there which emulate vintage instruments (vintage = old). *But* if you're new to computer music in general, and laptop music in particular, then you really shouldn't feel any need to follow the old ways – look at software and hardware that points forward, not stuff that looks back to a theoretical 'golden age', and if you are already using a computer/laptop for music, the same thing applies to you!

We're only scraping the surface of what's possible in terms of interface design; on-screen virtual knobs don't make sense. Propellerheads' Reason (www.propeller-heads.se) is incredibly popular, but the majority of people use it because it's a cheap alternative to 'real' equipment, not because of its sound or other attributes. This 'cheapness' on behalf of the user is why there are zillions of cracked copies of Reason floating around – people just want free stuff. Propellerheads might have trouble steering Reason into a 'be yourself' software future, where it's no longer necessary or desirable to emulate archaic hardware; in some ways, it has more use as an educational tool, teaching students how to patch hardware. Propellerheads have landed themselves with a product that's very hard to update – as computer displays take on increasingly 'widescreen' oriented formats, the vertically scrolling virtual rack is going to be hard to justify. I hope Propellerheads succeed; Reason functions very well, and sounds acceptable (especially with the addition of third-party or home-grown sounds); it's the interface that I object to.

Music apps which I've already mentioned in this book will define the future – performance/composition tools like Ableton Live (www.ableton.com) and radiaL (www.cycling74.com), and manipulation/sound design tools like Melodyne (www.melodyne.com).

Sonasphere (www.sonasphere.com) gives an indication of where future performance software might go – taking a step beyond Live and radiaL into a more experimental realm – doing away with traditional audio software design altogether. If you've got any feelings at all about this interface issue, you should see it. On the website they call it 'A sample-based live sound performance system with a generative 3D interface' – does that make everything clear?

The interface is a 3D environment where the various elements that comprise a set are represented as floating spherical objects. These elements can be sound samples, effects, or mixers. You have to make connections between these objects, and the parameters of the objects can be controlled by the 3-D co-ordinates of the other objects that they are connected to. There is also a 'generative mode', where the connections are made and edited automatically.

Quote

Much more flexible software to allow better integration between acoustic/ electric musos and electronic. SongCarver

Quote

Easy-to-remember menu combinations' never work on stage for me. One function, one button. That's it. SongCarver

Sonasphere diagram.

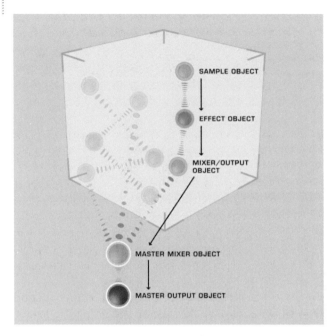

It's an interesting application, both sonically and visually – this could be a good one for live jamming if your laptop is connected to a PA and video projector at the same time. The only regret I have with Sonasphere is that it's crying out to be somehow manipulated in real space, instead of on a flat computer screen. Well somehow, someday.

And I nearly forgot to mention, Sonasphere is free at the moment, so if you're a Mac OSX user, why not go to the site and try it?

Video software like iMovie (www.apple.com) and Arkaos (www.arkaos.net) will become more important to musicians, as they realise their ability to deliver a full audio/visual performance/package; this will become the norm in the 'cottage industry' music business of the future.

- *Software will keep getting better. And people will keep mutating and mechanising their music beyond belief before realising that music theory actually makes it all sound better.* Lionel Valdellon

Performance

- *I'd like to see more laptops appearing in bands with other musicians and see what that adds to it.* mindlobster

Ableton Live will be on every laptop musician's computer. Elastic audio will reduce MIDI to a control protocol. Sampling will be everywhere, you can take any noise and pitch shift it, stretch it, generally brutalise it, and turn it into a top 40 hit (well maybe not that last part). Even plug-ins are less important, the choice of source sounds is all. Live will be the app that takes us there. I like to boast that I was one of its first users, and it just gets better. Everything else must be compared to it. There's still nothing to beat it. I love it.

- *As the home computer set the musician in the studio free from practising mechanical instruments, so will the laptop free the live performer.* Luke

- *Michael Jackson on stage with a PowerBook… just it becoming more common place for a laptop to be seen on stage with regular musicians —until something better comes along.* JDG

In conclusion

You can be swept away on a tidal wave of continuous updates, always absorbed in new things, and waiting for even newer things, or you can choose to opt out of the update race. There is no happy medium – if you update one app, or maybe your OS, then you are bound to be forced into other updates to keep your apps talking to each other. I would like to do it, to stop playing 'keep-up', but there's always some great new feature, or some bug fix, that you can't live without.

A matter of weeks after you bought it, your precious new laptop will be a piece of junk – something new will come along fast, get used to it! If it bothers you, the solution is easy – just stop looking at the websites and magazines that trade on the desire for new stuff.

There are people who talk of being tired of computers, bored with the internet – people who stop checking their e-mail and don't bother renewing their domain names. There are people I know who have given up on all that, and, even as Apple and Microsoft are pushing their 'digital hubs' with laptop/phone/PDA/diary synchronisation, they are returning to the Filofax that has lain dormant in their drawer for the past couple of years. So don't assume too much! Maybe laptop music will still exist in five years, broadly as it is now, or perhaps a company with enough resources at its disposal, such as Yamaha, or Roland, will create a revolutionary, portable product which combines the best of computer design with the best of 'traditional' music hardware. Let's see – it'll be fun. Until then, make the best music you can with what you've got!

- *I used to record my vocals into a VHS deck, and I wrote an entire musical on a battery operated sequencer. I used to sing a lot when I was out. I'd call my answering machine and sing, and then use that as a sample. I used to come home and get all these singing messages, and think 'who's that?* mindlobster

- *We shouldn't limit ourselves to just digital technology. The range of sounds that can be brought in once we introduce analogue technology and musical instruments into the equation is endless.* Ergo Phizmiz

- *I'm afraid the only thing that will arise is the outcome of tons of electronic music on laptops by people who bought a laptop because it became an affordable tool and because they use cracked software. But there's something positive too; more and more people are getting into constructing their own patches and it creates a nice working area. Often these people combine audio with video in a creative and nice domestic way, and it creates a nice vibe.*

  Maybe people will get fed up with 'laptopism' concerts or events, but I see the laptop becoming the number one audio source on stage. Is electronic music here to stay? For sure. So I don't see any reason for laptop music (whatever it is) to disappear. Eavesdropper

> **Quote**
>
> *I'm the future – hard core music/programming people getting into Linux music on laptops.* Brian Redfern

Laptop music links

www.aapspower.com – solar power systems for laptops
www.ableton.com – they make Ableton Live, the quintessential laptop music app
www.acer.com – laptop manufacturers
www.adobe.com – Audition editor (formerly CoolEdit)
www.agentsimon.com – VJ
www.akaipro.com – VZ8 sampler plug-in
www.alesis.com – AirFX performance effects
www.alsa-project.org – Advanced Linux Sound Architecture
www.alteclansing.com – inMotion iPod speaker system
www.aluminiumcases.com – can you guess?
www.ambrosia.com – Wiretap software
www.antarestech.com – plug-ins
www.apogeedigital.com – Mini-Me USB audio interface
www.apple.com – computers, Final Cut Pro, MacOSX, iMovie, iPod, iTunes, QuickTime, Soundtrack
www.aptwebsite.com – venue hosting regular iPod DJ events
www.arbiter.co.uk – distributors of hardware and software
www.arboretum.com – Hyperengine A-V media editing software
www.archos.com – external storage
www.arkaos.net – VJ software
www.arturia.com – Moog Modular V, Storm software
www.asapien.org – Brian Redfern, musician
http://audacity.sourceforge.net – free audio editor
www.audionerdz.com – plug-ins
www.audiotrak.co.uk – USB audio interfaces
www.audiovisualizers.com – VJ resource
www.avid.com – Avid Free DV video editing software
www.cix.co.uk/~tralala Beep, a Stylophone for PDA
www.belkin.com – iPod Voice Recorder, cases, and other computer accessories
www.bias-inc.com – Peak audio editor
www.bigbamboo.org.uk – 'Laptop Jam' documentary
www.bitheadz.com – Session synth/sampler
www.synthzone.com/bsynth – Body Synth – use your body movement to control MIDI
www.broadscape.net – provider of wifi services for public use
www.casedirect.com – Case Logic laptop cases
www.cddb – the CD Database, as used by iTunes
www.celemony.com – Melodyne software
www.chapmanstick.com – string instrument with option MIDI pickup
www.clieplaza.com – Sony Clie PDAs
www.compaq.com – laptop computers
www.cerlsoundgroup.org/continuum – like a giant ribbon controller!
www.contourdesign.com – USB editing controllers
www.crumpler.com – laptop cases

www.csounds.com – programming language for audio
www.cycling74.com – Pluggo effects, radiaL performance software, Max/MSP authoring software
www.daviddas.com – performer/producer
www.digidesign.com – MBox USB audio interface
www.digigram.com – VX Pocket PC Cardbus audio interface
www.digitalfishphones.com – plug-ins
www.dj1800.com – DJ software
www.eastpak.com – laptop cases
www.echoaudio.com – Indigo PC Cardbus audio interface
www.edirol.com – USB1/2 audio/MIDI interfaces and controllers
http://groups.yahoo.com/group/electronicamanila – collective of Filipino electronica artists
www.emagic.com – Logic sequencer, USB audio interfaces
www.emf.org – dedicated to the promotion of electronic music
www.ergophizmiz.com – performer/composer
www.esi-pro.com – Gigaport USB audio interface
www.evolution.co.uk – MIDI/USB keyboards and controllers
www.collective.co.uk/expertsleepers – XFade sample looping plug-in
www.finalscratch.com – deck-based controller for DJ use
www.five12.com – Numerology sequencer
www.fogscreen.com – see it to believe it
www.fraunhofer.de – creators and owners of the MP3 format
www.fruityloops.com – software sequencer
www.gdam.sourceforge.net – Geoff And Dave's Audio Mixer
www.girl.yowstar.com – Girl jamming app
www.greenoak.com – plug-ins, including Crystal synth
www.griffintechnology.com – the iMic USB audio interface
www.harmankardon.com – small speaker systems for computer use
www.magicandaccident.com – Matthew Herbert, musician
http://mmturner.home.mindspring.com – HostX VST plug-in host
www.goincase.com – In Case laptop cases
http://touchlab.mit/edu – information on haptics (ask SongCarver)
www.13941a.org – all about FireWire
www.image-ine.com – VJ software
www.indiefilipino.com – resource for Filipino musicians/artists
www.irez.com – USB and FireWire webcams
www.irixx.org – musician
www.jansport.com – laptop cases
www.jbl.com – Creature speaker systems
www.jlcooper.com – numerous control surfaces including CS-32 mini USB mixer
http://freesoftware.ircam.fr – jMax, free graphical programming environment

www.johnlewis.com – Windows/Mac computer dealers
www.robinjudge.com – musician
www.karrimor.com – laptop cases
www.kensington.com – USB lights
www.kentonuk.com – wireless MIDI system
www.keyfax.com – Phatboy MIDI controller
www.keyspan.com – Digital Media Remote
www.kinoray.com – VJ David De Saint
www.knobsounds.com – musician Eavesdropper
www.korg.com – Kaoss Pad performance effects unit, PXR4 digital studio
www.kurzweilmusicsystems.com – Expression Mate ribbon controller
www.kvr-vst.com – Zoyd synth plug-in
www.lacie.com – external storage – hard drives, and CD/DVD writers
www.laptop-jams.com – Brighton/London laptop jams
www.laptopmusic.com – nothing to do with this book!
www.linux.org – resource for all Linux-related info
www.linuxdj.org – self explanatory, I hope
www.linux-laptop.net – self explanatory, I hope
www.linuxsound.org – self explanatory, I hope
www.livepa.org – resource for live performance with laptops and sequencers
http://homepage1.nifty.com/tomo_ya/livesticks-e.html – Livesticks: game controller to MIDI
www.lowepro.com – laptop cases
www.macally.com – too many Mac-related items to list!
www.mackie.com – Spike USB audio interface
www.macromedia.com – Flash graphics software
www.m-audio.com – producers and distributors of HEAPS of laptop-friendly gear!
www.mda-vst.com – free (and great) VST plug-ins
www.mhlabs.com – Metric Halo FireWire audio interface
www.microsoft.com – ...it's Microsoft!
http://members.magnet.at/hubwin/midi.html – MIDI Joystick: game controller to MIDI
www.millennium-music.biz – build-to-order music laptops
www.mindlobster.com – performer and VJ
www.minimusic.com – music apps for PDAs
http://mixxx.sourceforge.net – Mixxx DJ software
www.mochipet.com – performer.
www.monyetas.com/creed – MidiKeys qwerty-to-MIDI application
www.motiondive.com – VJ software
www.motu.com – MOTU828 FireWire audio/MIDI interface
www.musicguard.co.uk – insurance
www.nanoloop.com – sequencer for GameBoy
www.nativeinstruments.com – music apps including Traktor DJ Studio
www.newertech.com – laptop batteries
www.noisefactoryrecords.com – musician Neil Wiernik
www.novationmusic.com – ReMOTE 25 controller/interface
www.nowax.co.uk – iPod DJ events in London
www.openjay.org – open source DJ software
www.orangemicro.com – how to add FireWire/USB2 to your older laptop
www.ozmusiccode.com – Alphabet Soup qwerty-based music app
www.pawfal.org – 'audio/visual foolishness for Linux'
www.pure-data.org – PD, free graphical programming environment
www.powerfx.com – samples online, on CD, on DVD; SoundShuttle VST sample browser
www.presonus.com – FireStation audio/MIDI interface\

www.propellerheads.se – Reason, Recycle, Rebirth
www.pspaudioware.com – plug-ins
www.publicloop.com – iBook-toting prison/community education project, using Live/Arkaos
www.rawmaterialsoftware.com – Tracktion sequencer
www.reasonstation.net – resource for Reason users
www.essl.at/works/replay.html – REplayPLAYer sound mangler
www.resonancefm.com – streaming 'alternative' radio station
www.rme-audio.com – Multiface/Hammerfall Cardbus audio interfaces
www.rogueamoeba.com – Audio Hijack software
www.roland.com – MIDI pickups for guitar, bass, and Chapman Stick
www.sagantech.biz – Metro audio/MIDI sequencer
www.samsonite.com – laptop cases
www.sleepbot.com – online ambient radio
www.slenderwhiteman.com – musician
www.smartdisk.com – external storage – hard drives, and CD/DVD writers
www.smartelectronix.com – fabulous Destroy FX plug-ins
www.sonasphere.com – ground-breaking performance software
www.songcarver.com – performer
www.sonicfoundry.com – Vegas media editing software
www.sonomic – online sample distribution
www.sonophile.com – DeKstasy DJ software
www.sony.com – it's Sony!
www.sospubs.co.uk – Sound On Sound, highly regard music technology magazine
www.soundbeam.co.uk – beam-based movement-to-MIDI interface
www.soundforge.com – audio editor
www.soundprofessionals.com – t-mics for minidisc recorders
www.spongefork.com – jamming-oriented synth/sampler
www.dfuse.com/sprawl – events curated by Douglas Benford
www.steim.org – Junxion joystick-to-MIDI utility
www.steinberg.net – Halion, D'Cota, Rewire, Remix, Cubase, etc
www.sub.co.uk – build-to-order music laptops
www.sumdex.com – laptop cases
www.suse.com – a version of Linux
www.tascam.com – USB audio/MIDI interfaces
www.tcelectronic.com – Spark editing software, PowerCore external effects device
www.theplaysthething.com – laptop-using composer Joe Young
www.emiliatelese.com – artist/performer
www.terminatorx.cx – Linux based music mangling
www.djcj.org – TerminatorX info
www.timbuk2.com – laptop cases
www.timeandspace.com – distributor of sample CDs
www.trolltouch.com – touchscreen displays for laptops
www.musork.com/trouble/ – information on Mochipet, Kit Clayton, Kid 606, and others
www.mochipet.com
www.tucano.it – laptop cases
www.ucapps.de – DIY MIDI control boxes
www.uisoftware.com – Videodelic VJ software
www.ultimatesupport.com – Ultimate Apex keyboard stand
www.vidvox.net – VDMXX VJ software
www.vjcentral.com – what it says
www.homepage.mac.com/underwoodaudio/disgrace – VJ Guineapigguano
www.warchalking.org – all about where to 'find' wifi networks
www.yamahasynth.com – sequencers, samplers, drum pads,
www.zoom.co.jp – PS-02 digital recorder

Index